Lombardi and Me

*Players, Coaches,
and Colleagues Talk about
the Man and the Myth*

Paul Hornung
with Billy Reed

TRIUMPH
B O O K S

Library of Congress Cataloging-in-Publication Data

Hornung, Paul, 1935–
    Lombardi and me : players, coaches, and colleagues talk about the man
    and the myth / Paul Hornung with Billy Reed.
      p. cm.
    ISBN-13: 978-1-57243-865-1 (hard cover)
    ISBN-10: 1-57243-865-7 (hard cover)
     1. Lombardi, Vince. 2. Fooball coaches—United States—Biography. I.
    Reed, Billy, 1943– II. Title.

GV939.L6H67 2006
796.332092—dc22
[B]
                                                              2006011664

This book is available in quantity at special discounts for your group or organization. For further information, contact:

Triumph Books
542 South Dearborn Street
Suite 750
Chicago, Illinois 60605
(312) 939-3330
Fax (312) 663-3557

Printed in U.S.A.
ISBN-13: 978-1-57243-865-1
ISBN-10: 1-57243-865-7
Design by Patricia Frey
All photos courtesy of Vernon Biever unless otherwise indicated. Photos on pages 138 and 140 courtesy of Bettmann/CORBIS. Photo on page 154 courtesy of AP/Wide World Photos.

With undying gratitude and love, I dedicate this book to Vince Lombardi. May his words, his values, and his legacy live forever.

Contents

Foreword
by Jeremy Schaap

In the locker room of the Green Bay Packers on the final day of 1961, players lounged around in various states of undress, killing time before the start of the National Football League's championship game. "Everybody look pretty," suggested end Max McGee. "There's gonna be 20 million people watching us on TV."

"How many of them are female?" a teammate wondered.

"Maybe five million."

"And The Horn knows half of them."

Private First Class Paul Vernon Hornung, on leave from Fort Riley, Kansas, grinned easily, conditioned to the kidding.

—Dick Schaap
from Paul Hornung: Pro Football Golden Boy

My father loved Paul Hornung, not the way Hornung loved women and they loved him, but he did love him. For my father—and millions of men of his generation—Paul Hornung was the ultimate jock: gifted, handsome, charming, funny, clutch. If Hornung had not been so damned likeable, it would have been easy to resent him. A decade before the ascent of Broadway Joe, the Golden Boy was the man every man wanted to be and every woman wanted to be with.

In 1962, six years before my father would write the best-selling *Instant Replay* with Jerry Kramer, the Packers' All-Pro right guard, he wrote a book about Hornung, who by then had played five seasons in the NFL. It was a modest effort—a 140-page paperback—but it showed flashes of brilliance. If nothing else, *Paul Hornung: Pro Football Golden Boy* captured the spirit of its subject and the spirit of the NFL as it was burgeoning into adulthood.

Leather helmets were out, but linemen were still of human proportions. No one on the Packers' offensive line weighed more than 250 pounds. Two-way players were gone, but two-career players were the rule. In the off-season, Hornung's teammates worked as salesmen and mechanics. Hornung was a notable exception to the rule. He worked 12 Sundays a year, plus playoffs. Yet no one begrudged him his exceptional status. He *was* exceptional, in every way, and denying it would have been pointless.

Hornung's irresistible aura was a familiar story by 1962. In the 70-plus-year history of the John W. Heisman Memorial Trophy, only once has the award been presented to a man who played for a team with a losing record. That was in 1956, when Paul Hornung of Notre Dame won the award. And the Irish weren't 5–6, or 4–5, or 4–6. They weren't just barely a losing team. They were 2–8.

"I couldn't believe it when they told me I'd won it," Hornung said. "I didn't think I was even up for consideration."

My father, then at *Newsweek*, shared Hornung's surprise. He had voted for the man who finished fifth in the balloting, Jim Brown, the Syracuse running back he had known since they were teenagers living in adjacent towns on Long Island. In fact, my father was so incensed that Brown did not win the Heisman—he thought Brown had been denied only because of his complexion—that he quietly boycotted the balloting for the next 25 years.

Hornung would later tell my father that he shared his disgust for the prejudice that cost Brown so many votes—which is not to say that he thought the wrong man won. That's one of the delightful things about Hornung. He is unabashedly immodest. False modesty would suit him no better than a Chicago Bears jersey. But he is not a braggart. He never had to be. Everyone else bragged about him, starting with Vince Lombardi, who called him the greatest player ever—inside the 20-yard line. "He could smell the end zone," Lombardi said, which I suppose made Hornung the sommelier of halfbacks.

Hornung's prettiness contrasted dramatically with his grittiness. Running out of bounds to avoid getting hit was anathema. His appetite for touchdowns was insatiable. "The best way to stop Hornung," an enemy lineman once said, "is to have 11 guys jump him all at once."

Hornung's greatness is one of those things that had to be witnessed. Today, while we have films and anecdotes that attest to his abilities as a ball carrier, most of the statistics tell a different story. In nine seasons in the NFL, he never rushed for more than 681 yards. (By way of comparison, Jim Taylor, Hornung's partner in the Packers backfield, rushed for more than 1,000 yards five straight seasons and for more than 700 yards seven straight seasons.) Only once did Hornung catch as many as 20 passes in a season.

Even adjusted for inflation—the NFL season has been lengthened from 12 games when Hornung was at his peak to 16—the numbers don't support the claims that Hornung was one of the all-time greats. Only once did he finish a season ranked among the top 10 in the league in rushing. That was 1960, when he finished seventh. This sentence appears alongside his statistics on Pro-Football-Reference.com, the definitive football website: "Paul Hornung is not in the all-time top 50 in any major category."

But.

There is one individual statistic that tells you all you need to know about Hornung: 176 points. In one 12-game season. An NFL record that still stands, despite the fact that the season is now 33 percent longer. What mattered to Hornung was winning—and you couldn't win without scoring.

On the other hand, training was decidedly not among those things that mattered to Hornung.

A few years after writing his Hornung biography, my father was back in Green Bay working on another story. By then, he was familiar with the lifestyle of prominent professional athletes. Hornung, though, was a breed apart. He made Mickey Mantle look like Mary Poppins. Shocked and awed by the quotidian details of the Golden Boy's existence, my father recorded them for posterity.

Each morning Paul would get up about quarter to 9:00 and be on the field by 9:00. They would practice until 12:00 and there would be meetings to 3:00. After 3:00 he'd come home, mix a pitcher of martinis, and drink martinis until 6:00 with Kramer and the others. Then they'd go out to dinner, a group of players. Scotch before dinner. Wine with dinner. Brandy after dinner. Then back to scotch. Every day. I lost count by the time it had reached more than 60 just how many drinks Paul had in that week leading up to the Browns game. Also, he never went to bed before 4:00 in the morning, he never went to bed alone, and he never repeated himself.

I am still uncertain how my father was able to confirm what he reported in that last sentence. And bear this in mind: anybody can party like that in New York or Los Angeles. But in Green Bay? For that, a special kind of dedication to dissolution was required.

Hornung has famously said that his epitaph should be: "He went through life on scholarship." There is an element of truth to that. Being Paul Hornung has been fun and rewarding, and off the field he has rarely had to sweat too hard. But it is also true that he has made good on his scholarship—with talent, grace, and charisma. Fifty years after he won the Heisman, his hair is now white, but Hornung remains golden.

Preface
by Billy Reed

Of all the men who have ever coached football, few have made a more profound impact on the game, their times, or the men they coached than Vince Lombardi. During his nine-year tenure with the Green Bay Packers (1959–1967), Lombardi did more than build and maintain one of the most colorful and efficient dynasties in the history of the National Football League. He became a folk hero, a cultural icon, a symbol of excellence and discipline and those elusive qualities that define greatness.

An immigrant's son, Lombardi was raised in Brooklyn, New York, as a devout Catholic. His religious convictions shaped everything he did and believed as a player at Fordham University, where he was a member of the famed "Seven Blocks of Granite" line, and as a coach at the high school, college, and pro levels. At West Point, where he served as an assistant under the legendary Col. Earl "Red" Blaik from 1949 to 1953, he learned discipline in the military sense. He was such an avid student of the game and of tactics, even to the point of analyzing Army game films with Gen. Douglas MacArthur, that he caught the attention of Wellington Mara, owner of the New York Giants, who hired him to be the team's top offensive assistant in 1954.

Because of his deep New York roots, Lombardi dreamed of becoming the Giants head coach. By 1958, it was obvious he was the heir apparent to Giants coach Jim Lee Howell. However, because Howell showed no intentions of retiring and Mara was notoriously reluctant to fire anybody, Lombardi accepted the Green Bay job when it was offered to him after the 1958 season. At the time, the Packers, located in the NFL's smallest market, were the laughingstock of the league. It took Lombardi only three seasons to get them into the NFL championship game.

The Packers won the NFL championship in 1961, 1962, 1965, 1966, and 1967. They won the first two Super Bowls, defeating Kansas City, champion of the American Football League, after the '66 season and Oakland the following year. Due to the growing influence of television, the Green Bay stars became national heroes. Everybody who knew anything about football knew something about Paul Hornung, Bart Starr, Jimmy Taylor, Ray Nitschke, Willie Davis, and all the others. But it was Lombardi, and the mystique that grew around him, that gripped a nation badly in need of trustworthy leaders and pillars of stability. The Packers dynasty, remember, coincided with the rise of the Vietnam War and the civil rights movement.

After the second Super Bowl victory, Lombardi shocked the football world by announcing his retirement. He probably knew the dynasty was crumbling because of age and attrition. However, he soon found that a desk in the front office wasn't for him. Like his old hero MacArthur, he was most at home on the battlefield. So in 1969 he left Green Bay to accept the head coaching job of the Washington Redskins.

For one glorious season, Lombardi was the toast of the nation's capital. He hobnobbed with the president of the United States, Richard Nixon, and the chief justice of the Supreme Court, Earl Warren, and other luminaries from the worlds of politics and show business. Interestingly, they all seemed more excited about being around Lombardi than he did about being around them. Naturally, he immediately turned the woebegone Redskins into a winner. Surely another dynasty was in the making. But then Lombardi was diagnosed with cancer. He died on September 3, 1970, at the age of 57.

This book is an attempt, however futile, to explain him through the words of the men who knew him best. What was it that set him apart? Why is he so widely quoted and revered to this very day? Why has the name Lombardi become virtually synonymous with not only winning, but doing it with a unique degree of excellence?

Acknowledgments

As Paul Hornung and I were working on his autobiography, *Golden Boy*, Paul said repeatedly that he wanted to do one more book. It would be about Vince Lombardi, his coach with the Green Bay Packers, and what he would do is interview the men who knew Lombardi best to see if they could define the elusive qualities that enabled Lombardi to mold championship teams out of ordinary talent and to squeeze every last drop of talent and potential out of every player he coached.

This book is Paul's dream made real.

It's safe to say that Lombardi and Hornung, the disciplinarian and the playboy, had one of the most interesting coach-player relationships in sports history. On a fundamental level, it was pragmatic: Hornung needed Lombardi to bring out the best in him, and Lombardi needed Hornung to win games. But it was more than that. Maybe Lombardi was the father Hornung, whose own dad abandoned him at a young age, never had. And maybe Hornung was the son of every father's dreams: handsome, charming, and blessed with extraordinary athletic ability.

Until their paths crossed in 1959, Hornung had not come close to living up to the national stardom he attained during his Heisman Trophy career at Notre Dame, and Lombardi had never been more than an assistant coach at either the college or pro levels. But one of Lombardi's first moves as the Green Bay coach was to put Hornung at left halfback, the star's position in his offensive scheme, and Hornung responded by becoming the leader, both on the field and in the locker room, that the Packers desperately needed.

For seven glorious seasons (not counting the 1963 season in which Hornung was suspended for betting on the Packers to win), Hornung was Lombardi's money player. Whenever the Packers got inside the 20-yard line, the coach depended on No. 5 to get points on the board somehow. The most versatile player in NFL history, Hornung could run, pass, catch, and place-kick. He also could throw a mean block. Lombardi frequently said that Hornung was the best "clutch player" he ever coached.

In return for being one of the main conduits between Lombardi and the players—one way or another, Lombardi frequently used Hornung to send messages to his teammates—Lombardi ignored the carousing that Hornung did with his trusty sidekick, Max McGee. Well, he didn't always ignore it. Whenever it reached a blatant level, Lombardi was forced to slap Hornung with a fine or give him a chewing-out. But everybody knew the coach loved Hornung as a father loves a mischievous son.

Undoubtedly, one of the hardest moments in Lombardi's career came soon after the 1966 season, when he told Hornung that he was putting him in the expansion draft that the NFL was holding to stock the new franchise in New Orleans. It was strictly business, and Hornung understood that Lombardi really had no choice. Hornung's best days were behind him, he was crippled by injuries, and Lombardi had a talented heir in Donny Anderson. Hornung tried to make it easy on his coach, talking about the money he could make—and the fun he could have—in New Orleans. But nobody was fooled, especially Lombardi.

In selecting the men he wanted to interview for this book, Hornung had only one criterion: they had to have known Lombardi on a very personal level. He made an exception for David Maraniss only because he was captivated by how well the author captured Lombardi in his book about the coach. Otherwise, the men he interviewed knew Lombardi well enough to shed some light on the qualities that made him unique among coaches and, yes, among men.

Paul and I are grateful to everyone who consented to be interviewed. We hope we accurately portrayed the devotion and gratitude that each feels to Coach Lombardi. We also are deeply indebted to Tom Bast, Jessica Paumier, and all the other talented editors, researchers, and designers at Triumph Books. They took our raw material and put it together in a way that we hope does justice to Coach Lombardi.

In addition, Paul would like to thank his wife, Angela, for her love, support, and patience, and I would like to thank a special friend, Martha McMahon, for her incredible loyalty.

We also would like to thank the greatest fans in football, the Green Bay Packers fans. Of all the fans of all the teams in the NFL, they are the most special—and the most deserving to have had Vince Lombardi as a big part of their legacy.

—Billy Reed

Introduction
by Paul Hornung

"It's a reality of life that men are competitive and the most competitive games draw the most competitive men. ... There is something in good men that really yearns for, needs, discipline and the harsh reality of head-to-head combat. I don't say those things because I believe in the 'brute' nature of man or that men must be brutalized to be combative. I believe in God, and I believe in human decency. But I firmly believe that any man's finest hour—his greatest fulfillment to all he holds dear—is that moment when he has worked his heart out in a good cause and lies exhausted on the field of battle, victorious."

—Coach Vince Lombardi

In the fall of 2004, I spent a lot of time promoting my second book, *Golden Boy*, an autobiography that I did with writer William F. Reed, an old friend who we know in Kentucky as "Billy." The book did well nationally, but it sold particularly well in the Midwest in general and Wisconsin in particular. Packers fans, bless their hearts, just can't seem to get enough of the franchise and its heroes, both past and present.

At one book-signing appearance after another, people always asked me about Vince Lombardi. Although Coach has been dead more than 30 years, there's still an amazing amount of interest in him. He has become a true legend. So the questions come: What was he really like? What made him special? Over and over, I got the same questions everywhere I went.

So it dawned on me that maybe I should do one last book and that it should attempt to answer all those questions about Lombardi. I thought about it a lot. On the other hand, there already are a lot of Lombardi books out there. His son, Vince Jr., did an especially good one, and I thought David Maraniss did a terrific job in his book, *When Pride Mattered: The Story of Vince Lombardi*. But nobody had done a book like the one I envisioned. I wanted the public to hear about Lombardi from the people who knew him best: his former players.

I didn't have any trouble selling my friend, Tom Bast, on publishing the book or in convincing Billy Reed to work with me again. The hardest part was picking the people to interview. Naturally, I wanted to lean heavily on my former teammates with the Packers, beginning with Bart Starr, who was an extension of Lombardi on the field. Bart was the perfect quarterback for Lombardi. Not even a Johnny Unitas or a Joe Namath would have been better for the Packers.

Unquestionably, I had to include my old running buddies. Max McGee was my best friend and partner in crime with the Packers, and our two great guards, Jerry Kramer and Fuzzy Thurston, did a lot of pulling and blocking for us off the field as well as on it. Forrest Gregg and Bill Curry each have a unique perspective on Lombardi, and I wanted to include Willie Davis and Marv Fleming to speak for the African American players. Because of Lombardi, our teams had a sense of closeness that enabled us to beat teams with more raw talent. We loved each other. It's as simple as that.

Before he came to Green Bay, Lombardi was an assistant on the great New York Giants teams of the 1950s, so I got Frank Gifford and Sam Huff to talk about what he was like in those days. Huff also worked for Vince in the year he spent coaching the Redskins. Along with Sonny Jurgensen and Larry Brown, he shares a lot of memories about Lombardi's last job.

As you read the book, you will see that all the former players have a favorite personal Lombardi story or a unique bit of insight into what made him special. Interestingly, however, you also will see some recurring themes, such as his "single-mindedness of purpose."

As good as the former players were, I also wanted to get the perspective of others who had a different relationship with the coach. So I interviewed his son, Vince Jr., and George Dixon, who knew Lombardi for years and coached under him at Washington. I talked Jeremy Schaap into doing a foreword about the relationship between his late father, Dick, and Lombardi. Dick loved our Packers teams and ghostwrote a book for me long before he teamed with Jerry Kramer to do the classic *Instant Replay*.

I even found some quotes from the late Henry Jordan about Lombardi, and I put them in a chapter as a way of honoring the great Packers who are no longer with us. Henry was more than a teammate. He and I were in the National Guard together.

I also interviewed a couple of writers—Lee Remmel, who spent decades covering the Packers for the *Green Bay Post-Gazette*, and Maraniss, who knew Lombardi only from the research he did for his book. Each told me some things I didn't know, as did Jack Koeppler, a Green Bay insurance man who played a lot of golf with Lombardi and knew him on a private, away-from-football level.

Surprisingly, I found that the toughest interview of all was me.

It has often been said that Vince and I had a father-son relationship, and there's more truth in that than anybody will ever know. We constantly tested each other, just as a father and son would. I tried to see how far I could push him and what I could get away with, and he tried to see how much of his discipline I could take. He told me once, "I'm going to get on your ass because you need it, but also because you can take it and some of the others can't." Many times, he might have been chewing me out, but he was really trying to reach somebody else who couldn't have taken it.

Vince changed my life, and he came along at just the right time. My first two years with the Packers were so unhappy and unsatisfying that I was ready to quit and do something else. My options ranged from going to Hollywood to make movies to returning home to Louisville to go into business with my uncle, Henry Hoffman, and my dear friend, Frank Metts. I doubt seriously that I would have been very happy, or lasted very long, doing either one. I needed a sense of purpose and direction in my life to keep me from drifting, and that's exactly what Lombardi gave me.

He told me right away that I was going to be his left halfback, just as Gifford had been in New York. No more would I have to keep switching positions. And he told me that if I didn't make it playing left halfback for him, I would not make it in pro football. Simple as that. That challenge motivated me and gave me the focus I needed. From then on, I was committed to being the best professional football player I could be.

Near the end of my career, Vince and I were having a talk. Just the two of us. We did that often. Whenever I had a problem or needed advice, I'd always go to Vince. This time he told me, "You've done something no football player has ever done. You won the Heisman Trophy in college as a quarterback and you were named Most Valuable Player in the NFL as a halfback." I could tell he was proud of me. His comments that day meant as much to me as when he told reporters that I was the best clutch player he ever coached.

Try as I might, I can't quite put my finger on one quality that set Vince apart from anybody else, but I think it's something he found inside himself and developed when he was on Col. Red Blaik's staff at West Point in the late 1940s and early 1950s. I think that Col. Blaik probably was the Vince Lombardi of his time.

Every Sunday during the season, one of Lombardi's duties was to take the game film of the Army game to Gen. Douglas MacArthur at his apartment at the Waldorf-Astoria Towers in New York City. Then he would sit with MacArthur and go over the films with him. Imagine that if you can: Douglas MacArthur and Vince Lombardi in a dark room studying football film. I would have loved to be a fly on the wall in that room.

When you stop and think about it, football and the army are pretty much the same thing. Sports and the army, for that matter. When you think about coaches such as Bear Bryant, Adolph Rupp, Tom Landry, Dean Smith, Bob Knight, Mike Krzyzewski, and Bill Parcells, the first things you think about are discipline, hard work, execution, organization, preparation, and attention to detail. It's the army way, and it certainly was Lombardi's way. He believed that if you did all those things, winning was inevitable. And make no mistake—winning was what Lombardi was all about.

In his chapter in this book, Jerry Kramer mentions that he once inscribed a book to Lombardi by saying, "To Coach Vincent Thomas Lombardi, a man against whom all others will be measured." That gets it pretty well. All of us who were touched by Lombardi were defined by him. He taught us how to win, and the winning gave us an identity that each of us has carried through life.

I never really said good-bye to the coach. I couldn't. The last time I saw him, maybe a month before his death, he was optimistic and looking forward to the season and talking about what a helluva passer Jurgensen was. How could I not play along? How could I tell him that I knew we would not see each other again in this life?

Doing this book has been a labor of love for me. A love for football, for the era in which I played, and for the guys I played with and against. But mostly, a love for Vince Lombardi. After all these years, he still lives in the hearts of all of us. I hope this book does a little bit to explain why.

Lombardi and Me

CHAPTER 1

Vince Jr. on Growing Up Lombardi

When I was young, it used to bother me, being Vince Lombardi Jr. You don't know any better when you're young. You don't realize it is what it is, and it's not your problem, and you can handle it any way you wish. But when I'm not out there being Vince Lombardi Jr., I'm hiding down here in Virginia and I don't want any part of it. I get all kinds of invitations to things because of my name, but I'm just not going to do it.

Don't misunderstand me. I make a good living making motivational speeches, and I know it's the name that does it. So, number one, it pays the bills. Number two, I've got something to say. It's his message, and it's still as vital today as it was, well, since the beginning of the country. You know, the ideas of discipline, sacrifice, and paying the price. We don't hear enough of that kind of stuff. It's easy to talk about it because I grew up with it. It's all I know.

I speak to a lot of businesses because there's a parallel that business sees in football. Football is a good model that you can somehow transfer to the business world. A lot of the kids they hire today are bright, but they don't want to work hard. They have no concept of what it's like to work within a team. They don't understand that sometimes you've got to give it up for the good of the whole.

> **Being a coach wasn't enough for my dad. He had to be a teacher. He had to be a molder of men.**

When I was born in 1942, my dad was teaching and coaching at St. Cecilia's in New Jersey. Looking back now, the amazing thing to me is that besides coaching football he also taught physics, chemistry, and Latin. And he coached a basketball team that won a state championship even though he didn't know a thing about the game.

I remember when we lived at West Point in the late 1940s and early 1950s. Dad loved West Point. Col. Blaik was the Army coach then, and he was probably the single biggest influence on my dad as a coach.

Every Sunday, Col. Blaik would tell Dad to take the game film down to the Waldorf Towers in New York City so Gen. MacArthur could look at it. My dad thought Gen. MacArthur was pretty special. Not everyone did, because MacArthur had defied President Truman, but Dad loved him. He loved everything about West Point. He believed in duty, honor, country. West Point felt right to him.

The cheating scandal happened when we were there. Some of the cadets on the football team were cheating on their tests and their buddies wouldn't rat on them, which was a violation of the cadet code. Col. Blaik's son was one of those who got caught and thrown out. Dad just never understood it. He couldn't figure out why. I mean, you don't rat on a buddy.

Living at West Point was pretty good, because you got a lot of perks. But he gave that up to go to work for the Giants. He had to get a second job to make ends meet. He was selling insurance and working for a factory somewhere. He wasn't making a lot of money, and my mom could spend it. I remember some disagreements over money, but my mom paid all the bills and I'm not sure he even remembered half the time. All he thought about, really, was football.

My dad was a perfectionist, and that's positive in many respects, but when you're his kid it doesn't take much to set off the perfectionist.

Something's out of line and—wow!—off they go. And you never know when it's going to happen so you're always walking around on eggshells. You just never knew what was going to set him off.

He'd come home for dinner, even during the season, and we'd sit around the table, but it wasn't a family conversation. My mother was dying to know what was going on and she would ask him, but he just didn't talk much about it.

I thought he didn't care about me. But after I became a parent, I understood what he was doing. He cared, but, like a lot of men of that time, he wasn't into showing it. He was tough on me. If he had really given my football his full attention, I couldn't have stood the pressure.

He was tough on his players, too. There were times when he would get angry and jump somebody. But he also would let the player know that, first, it wasn't personal, and second, he'd quickly find a way to repair it. You know, pat them on the back or do something to let them know he still loved them. A lot of folks don't realize they've done it and they don't repair the fence, and over time it becomes something bigger.

My dad would find me the dirtiest, rottenest summer jobs he could. I worked in a pickle factory, did construction. In the middle of summer he'd come to me and say, "Do you want to go to training camp?" And naturally I'd say yes, just to get out of whatever job I was doing. He paid me a few bucks to shag practice balls or whatever. The neat thing was, my mother thought I was in the training camp dorm at night and my dad thought I was home, and usually I was neither.

When I was in high school, my dad wanted me to go to West Point very badly. But my grades—at least in math—were not very good. He made me take Algebra II, and even though I passed it he didn't think my grades were good enough, so he made me take it again my senior year. At West Point in those days, you had to take all those basic engineering courses, and there's no way I could have handled that. Just no way. I knew that in my heart of hearts.

So dad was going to send me to a prep school, St. Thomas in St. Paul, Minnesota, and all that crap, but I told him I wanted to go someplace where I could major in phys ed and become a coach. But he looked at me and said, "That's okay, but if you do I'm not putting one penny toward your education." He didn't want me to be a coach, see? I thought he was yanking my chain, but I wasn't sure.

I had a chance to go to Dartmouth. I was recruited. But the Ivy League didn't give athletic scholarships, so when I told him what the tuition was he said, "Oh, shit." It was probably $15,000 a year back then. No way he was going to pay that much for me to go to Dartmouth. So I ended up at the College (now University) of St. Thomas in Minnesota, where I got a scholarship to play football. I was a fullback, and I had a decent career.

After my freshman year, I forgot to reserve a dorm room for the following year. So I report back for football in the fall and I don't have a room on campus. A bunch of us football players got a house off campus. Well, I called home and mentioned that as an "Oh, by the way…" sort of thing. The next morning he calls the dean of men and tells him to send me home because I was living off campus, which was against the rules.

The dean of men called me in. He was a priest, a tough guy, who had been in the air force. I was embarrassed to death, but he found me a room on campus. I wasn't too happy about it, but it was the best thing for me. I made the dean's list both semesters that year. Of the four guys I was going to room with, two were back on campus by the second semester, one never graduated, and the other one took six years to graduate. My father knew me better than I did.

Once when I was playing football in college, I got a bad knee. So I went to Minneapolis, where the Packers were playing, and asked Dad if I could see the Packers' team doctor. The doctor manipulated my knee and said, "It's just loose." Dad got furious. He thought I was faking it. He got in my face and screamed, "You're going to run on that thing *tomorrow!*" So the next day, I ran on that thing. Two weeks later, I was back in the starting lineup.

Vince Lombardi Jr. delivers his father's message through motivational speaking and helping others succeed in life by reaching their potential as both professionals and human beings. Photo courtesy of AP/Wide World Photos.

He was the same way with his players. In those days, a guy wanted to play even if he was hurt, because he didn't want to lose his job. There were only half as many teams as there are today, and the backups were just about as good as the starters. Today some of them want to play, but most of them don't want to let an injury jeopardize and shorten their careers. So it's a whole new dynamic today.

Doctors have changed, too. In Dad's era, the doctors took their orders from the coach. That's not the case anymore because they're all worried about malpractice suits. They're a lot more careful now than they were then.

When I was getting ready to go to law school, he thought for sure I would go to Marquette. It was in Milwaukee, so I would have been close to him in Green Bay. He was shocked when I went to Minnesota instead. But I was in love with this girl who was there. I eventually married her, and we had three kids while I was in law school.

When you're only a generation removed from immigrant status, as my dad was, you want your son to be a professional. For my dad, that meant being a lawyer. So I did what he wanted me to do, as usual. I went to law school and I hated it. I absolutely hated it. But I did it to please Dad.

Sometimes he would confide in me. After the Packers beat the Cowboys in the famous "Ice Bowl" game of 1967, we were driving away from the stadium and my dad said to me, "You just saw me coach my next-to-last game." That was news. I don't think anybody else knew besides my mom. I just think he was worn out, so he made that decision to retire. He announced it a few days after the Super Bowl. He was depressed and he just wasn't himself. He was just run down and fatigued.

But he had a great off-season, and when training camp started in the fall, he realized he had made a mistake. He couldn't come back to Green Bay, because Phil Bengston had succeeded him and that wouldn't be fair to Phil. So he just bided his time until Edward Bennett Williams came along and offered him the Redskins job. Williams was a big-shot Washington attorney and a good friend of Dad's.

It was a great opportunity for Dad. I'm sure being in Washington, D.C., had a lot to do with it. But so did the money. Williams gave Dad the chance to buy 15 percent of the team, which he did, even though he had to borrow to do it. After Dad died, Williams bought the 15 percent back from Mom. I guess she could have made a lot of money if she had kept it, but she also might have had trouble paying off the loan.

By the time I got out of law school, my dad had taken the job with the Redskins. I'd taken the bar exam but didn't know if I'd passed it.

My wife and I had just had our third child, so Dad said that we should move to Washington and that Edward Bennett Williams would get me a job with the justice department or something.

> **My dad was a perfectionist, and that's positive in many respects, but when you're his kid it doesn't take much to set off the perfectionist.**

By the time we got there, the team was in training camp in Carlisle, Pennsylvania, and Dad didn't have time to get involved. I talked with Edward Bennett Williams, but nothing materialized. So I went to downtown Washington and got a job with a law firm on my own. I had to commute an hour in and an hour out, and my dad always was growling at me because I wasn't there to hold open the door for my mother and everything. So we just up and went back to Minnesota, and they were not happy about it.

I remember one time during that period, my dad and I were driving together in downtown Washington. He turns to me and says, "You think I made a mistake taking the Redskins job?" I hadn't thought about it much one way or the other, and I told him so. But that question told me he had some doubts of his own.

I didn't see Dad much after I moved back to Minnesota. I remember one time, though, when I was in New York and I took a Greyhound down to Washington to see Dad. So I'm standing outside the bus terminal in Washington, D.C., not in a very good part of town, and Dad sends his limo to pick me up. I'm sure everybody thought, "Whew, that must be Mr. Greyhound." But other than that, about the only times I saw him were when he was in the hospital or home recuperating.

My life changed in 1975, about five years after Dad died, when I got into football by taking a job with the Seahawks. I was miserable until then. But from that day until now, I've never again sat around on a Sunday and said, "Oh, Jesus, tomorrow's Monday and I have to go to work in the law office." I've had 15 or 16 different jobs, and most of those changes, including politics and everything, was a matter of trying to avoid the practice of law.

I'm asked all the time if I think my dad could win today, with the players and the game having changed so much. I think he would have adjusted and modified the Xs and Os part of it, but that basically his system would have worked today. I also think it would have been tougher to find the kind of guys who would respond to him. But I firmly believe that most guys want to win, and if you give them a chance to win, they will modify themselves so they will win. With my dad, they would have won, unless they're somebody like Terrell Owens. I don't know if he wants to win bad enough to have played for Dad. But Dad's way was pretty simple: if we lose you're gone.

He would think that football today is a whole lot more complicated than it needs to be. They've got so many coaches today that they even have assistant special teams coaches, and they're paying them a lot of money. I guess the feeling is that the talent pool isn't as good as it used to be so they're going crazy on paying coaches, figuring the best ones will find a way to win even with mediocre talent.

Being a coach wasn't enough for my dad. He had to be a teacher. He had to be a molder of men. I've always thought he would have been much happier coaching at the college level than the NFL. I think he would have had more opportunities to teach and mold.

Looking back, I think the reason he took the Redskins job had more to do with power than money. If he had lived and the Redskins had had some success, I think he could have had some influence on this country's direction, at least indirectly. I'm not saying that Congress or the president or heads of state would have listened to him one-on-one, but he would have been in the newspapers talking about commitment and discipline and sacrifice. It was Washington, D.C., you know, so his influence could have been wider than just football. But we'll never know.

Hornung on Lombardi Jr.: I can't imagine anything worse than being the son and namesake of a famous man. When your name is Vince Lombardi Jr., how can you ever hope to have your own identity? If I had ever had a son, I wouldn't have named him Paul Hornung Jr. It's just too much baggage to carry through life.

But "Little Vince," as I call him, has done all right for himself. His dad wanted him to become a lawyer, so he did. Before Vince Sr. died, he got to see his son in a three-piece suit. "Well, at least you look like a lawyer," the old man said. That was his way. It meant he was very proud.

Vince Jr. didn't go into football until after his dad died. He worked in the front office of the Seattle Seahawks, spent some time on the NFL's Management Council, and gave the USFL a try before it folded. Today he's a motivational speaker who draws heavily on the lessons he learned from his dad. He gets $10,000 or so a pop, so he's doing pretty well.

As he has gotten older, Vince Jr. has gotten to look and sound like his dad. It's almost eerie to be around him.

CHAPTER 2

Bart Starr: Lombardi's Leadership Was Turning Point for Pack

I didn't have much of a résumé when I came out of college. My junior year at Alabama, I had a bad back. I played very, very little. My senior year, we had a coaching change. Coach Bryant came in for Ears Whitworth, and he benched most of our seniors for the majority of the season. We didn't play that much.

Had it not been for a gentleman named Johnny Dee, who was the basketball coach at Alabama, I probably wouldn't have been drafted at all. He was a good friend of Jack Vainisi, the player/personnel director for the Packers at that time, and he leaned all over Vainisi to take a look at me.

No disrespect to the coaches at Green Bay prior to Lombardi, but the team was not well organized. When Lombardi came in there, you immediately recognized that what we were lacking was leadership. Scooter McLean, who was the coach before Lombardi, would sit down and play cards with some of the players the night before a game. It was that kind of atmosphere that was very unproductive for everybody.

The first time I met with Lombardi, I was just blown away. It was so powerful, how he opened and what he had to say. After about 40 minutes, we took a break and I ran downstairs and got on the phone and called Sherri back in Alabama. All I said to her was, "Honey, we're going to begin to win." We knew it immediately.

At the time Lombardi arrived, I was just trying to hang on, and it didn't look good for me when he traded for Lamar McHan. I think he felt Lamar was going to be his leader. At first he did all the talking in our quarterbacks meetings. We had to earn his trust, and that took some time. We had to learn to do things exactly as he wanted before he would lean on us for comments and so forth. He believed that you don't ever give trust away; it has to be earned.

He started McHan in the first game of his first season. We hadn't been winning and he had made the trade for McHan, so he was going to start there. But over time, I began to earn his trust and respect in practice. I proved to him that I could handle myself. So he made the change and started me, but I had to earn it first.

I think the turning point in my relationship with Coach Lombardi was after I became the starter. He would jump down my throat if I threw an interception in practice. I mean, all over me. I remember once I had a ball tipped in practice and then it was intercepted. And he just reamed me there in front of the guys.

I said, "Coach, may I see you in your office after we come off the field?" So I went in to see him and I said, "Coach, I can take the chewing out. You know by now that I can handle it. But you're chewing me out and demeaning my ass in front of the team that you're expecting me to lead. You'll see that you made a mistake about that tipped ball, but you'll apologize to me here in the office, not in front of the team. So if you want to chew me out, do it in the privacy of this office." I think I began to have a different kind of relationship with him at that point. He never chewed me out like that again in front of the team.

I grew up in a military family. My father was a master sergeant. I've told people many times that compared to my father, Lombardi was a piece of cake. People roll their eyes whenever I say that, but it's true. So I'm grateful for that because a lot of people couldn't handle Coach Lombardi personally, but I could.

If you couldn't take it, sometimes he'd get to you through somebody else. We had a couple of linemen that he could just chew their fannies out and another couple who couldn't take it. They'd go crawl in a hole if he chewed them out like that.

Other NFL quarterbacks have had more talent than Bart Starr, but under Lombardi the Packers field general became one of the greatest leaders the league has ever seen. Photo courtesy of AP/Wide World Photos.

The first time I met with Lombardi, I was just blown away.

In the nine years that you and I played together, Paul, I don't think he called nine plays in those nine years because we knew what he wanted. We knew exactly what he wanted us to audibilize to because he was very rigid in saying, "If you get this [defense], I want you to go to that [play]."

He was very aggressive, obviously, but he was very sound fundamentally, and he wanted to take advantage of audibles. We had a very simple system, terminology-wise, but the complexity of it was to kill the opponents because of our audibles, I think. They never knew when we were audibilizing because we never changed the tone or inflection of our voice. Hell, we could audibilize against our defense in practice and they didn't know it.

You guys, the backs and ends, were very, very helpful to me because I would ask you on the way back to a huddle if you could beat a linebacker or a defensive back on something. Is he covering you too far outside? Can you come back underneath him? You were all very astute and sharp about that, and it really helped me.

I didn't have the passing talent that a lot of these quarterbacks today have, but our running game enhanced my abilities. You, Paul, and Jimmy Taylor and our offensive line let me audibilize and call play-action passes. We were very, very effective because of that. We had the whole package.

It was a joy to play for him. I couldn't wait to go to the next meeting after a practice session and hear what he had to say and so forth. It was a great growth process for all of us.

We won five championships in seven years, and I've often been asked which was our best team. That's tough, but it would have been between the '62 team and the '66 team.

The first Super Bowl against the Kansas City Chiefs, Coach Lombardi's first comments as we began preparation for them was that he was very proud of us being able to represent the prestigious

National Football League in this first game. But then he quickly turned and said that the Chiefs were a very, very good football team and that we were going to have to be well prepared to beat them. He never let us take anybody for granted.

I coached the Packers from 1975 through 1983 and, in hindsight, I never should have taken the job. I knew better. I was a dumbo, and my inexperience hurt us all. Had I been prepared to be a coach, we could have turned it around.

Our offense always was well prepared. We could score against anybody. But we couldn't stop anybody. That's what killed us. We hadn't drafted for whatever it took to build a defense cohesively.

Sherri and I spent 31 years living in Green Bay. We even stayed there in the off-season. One of the reasons I love my wife so is that not one time in 31 years did she ever complain about the winters in Green Bay—and she despised it. But the people in Green Bay made it worthwhile. They are so great and wonderful. When Coach Lombardi turned it around so quickly, everyone turned with me. The fans just embraced everyone on the team.

Of course, it was very difficult for a black guy to find a place to live in those days. There just wasn't much of a black population, so it was tough on them. But if they weren't thrilled about coming to Green Bay initially, I think they got caught up in the winning and the excitement of the people. And Lombardi wouldn't allow even a hint of prejudice.

I remember once when Sherri was in downtown Green Bay shopping at Frankies, which is what we called the H.C. Frank & Co. department store. Our son must have been about two and a half, maybe three. He was walking around with her. And so the saleslady comes over and she sees Bart Jr. and she says, "I know who your daddy is." And Bart Jr. looks at her and says, "Paul Hornung." He used to idolize Paul. I think Lombardi did, too. You were a great clutch performer. Totally dedicated to the team and very unselfish. You worked as hard, or harder, than anybody in practice. I think that's why Coach Lombardi admired you so much.

I've told people many times that compared to my father, Lombardi was a piece of cake.

A lot of people aren't aware of the great sense of humor Lombardi had. One year after we played the Lions on Thanksgiving Day, he was going hunting the next day with his buddies up north. We gave him this T-shirt that said, on the front, "Italian Hunting Shirt." You turn it around and there was a great big bull's-eye on the back of it. His buddies said he couldn't show off that T-shirt enough.

And his emotions—he could cry very easily. After he left Green Bay, he came out in the early summer of '69 to play some golf with his buddies. We had a new home and he came over to visit us. Sherri took him on the tour, and then he came back to sit down in the den for a few minutes. He was praising Sherri for the job she had done, and she said, "Well, Coach, you're the one who made this possible…we wouldn't be here, except for you."

And he tears up immediately and walks over and gives her a big hug. When he turned around, he had tears running down his face. He came over and hugged me, and then he turned around and walked right out the door.

Hornung on Starr: Bart was the 17th pick in the 30-round draft coming out of college, and he was going nowhere in Green Bay until Lombardi got there. Under Lombardi, Bart became one of the great leaders in the history of the NFL. Other quarterbacks had stronger arms and better stats, but nobody was better than Bart at being an extension of the coach on the field.

Bart was a soft-spoken southerner, but he was tough as nails in the huddle. He knew exactly what Lombardi wanted, and he demanded that we execute the plays just as we had been taught them. Everybody in the stadium knew what we were going to do. But we did it so well, game after game, that it became almost impossible to stop us.

Lombardi loved Bart. They had that special relationship that only a coach and his quarterback can have. Years after Vince's death, Bart got a chance to coach the Packers. But as perfectly as he understood the Xs and Os part of Lombardi's mind, Bart lacked Vince's ability to inspire and motivate. That's no knock on Bart. No other coach, at Green Bay or anywhere else, has ever been able to be another Vince.

CHAPTER 3

Frank Gifford on the Giant in Vince

We were 3–9 in the 1953 season and I was ready to quit. I was making $8,250 a season, and I was playing both ways, both offense and defense. By the end of that year I had lost about 20 pounds and I was pretty beat up and discouraged. I knew I could do a lot better financially in the studios out in L.A. Plus, I wanted to go back and get my degree, which I eventually did.

But in the early spring of 1954, I got a call from Wellington Mara, the Giants owner. We talked a little bit, and he said he really wanted me to come back. I had gotten to know Wellington, a great guy, so I listened. He told me they had made Jim Lee Howell the head coach and they were bringing in some guy named Vince Lombardi to be the offensive coach. So I decided to come back. I had nothing to lose, really, so I went to training camp that summer in Salem, Oregon.

When I walked into the hotel lobby, he was standing there. I thought, "Who is this guy?" He came up and gave me that big smile and introduced himself. "I'm Vince Lombardi," he said, "and you are my halfback." From that point on, I never saw another moment of defense. He came in and took me off defense, and three years later I'm the Most Valuable Player in the National Football League.

Lombardi had been coaching at West Point, and it was obvious he didn't understand the professional game. The first thing he did was put in this nonsensical quarterback option play, and we struggled with that through the first two or three weeks of training camp. We used to laugh at him behind his back. We'd go out and have our beers after practice, and everybody would be imitating him. We called him "the Little General" and stuff like that.

One day at practice he had an orange peel. It was hot and we were tired, so pretty soon guys were getting sloppy and jumping offside. Stuff like that. So finally he put the orange peel down on the ground and said, "Nobody in front of the orange peel...nobody in front of the orange peel." And that night somebody stood up on the bar and shouted, "Nobody in front of the orange peel." And it became a thing we'd do every time he'd go off on a rant.

One night we were in Salem, Oregon, and he walked into the room I was sharing with Charley Conerly, our quarterback. He said, "What am I doing wrong?" He was very sincere, so we began talking to him. I said more than Charley. But Charley brought up that quarterback option play and said, "It won't work up here...can't run that." And we also told him that he didn't have to yell and scream all the time.

He listened very carefully. I mean, Charley Conerly was in the Marines four years in World War II. He fought at Guadalcanal, Iwo Jima, places like that. We had about a half dozen guys like that, and you didn't yell at them. You didn't yell at Charley Conerly. You just didn't. And Vince got the message.

He was very intelligent. When he was with us, some of the guys playing for him were older than he was. So he had to learn how to coach them to survive. He didn't have to change too much because we already were winning and we got along great. We really loved each other. So what he did was mix in some of his offense with what we already had. He put in maybe half a dozen plays, but he had every one down to a science.

He got rid of the guys who couldn't win, and then he became one of the guys with the rest of us. I had an apartment at the Concourse Plaza Hotel, and after a home game I'd have eight, 10, 12 guys come over. Sometimes Vince would come. He got along fine with Charley, and he liked Kyle Rote. He'd even go out with us when we went out on the town at night. He had to go that direction. When he went with you guys (the Packers), he went another direction.

> *He became kind of a big shot. He was the toast of the town, and everyone knew he was the brains behind our offense.*

After a while, it became obvious that he was a better coach than Jim Lee Howell, our head coach. So was Tom Landry, who took over as the Giants' defensive coach while he was still an active player. Howell had been a Marine lieutenant, and he was a great conditioning guy. He ran our ass off and got us in great condition. He didn't really have a clue what football was about, but he was smart enough to let Vince and Tom Landry, who was in charge of our defense, have their heads. He stayed out of the way, he really did. He had nothing to do with the offense, and little or nothing to do with the defense, just one area. With Lombardi, it was like he was the sergeant who should have been the general.

I got very close to Vince in the five years he was with the Giants. Charley and I used to go over to his house in New Jersey and look at game films. He got rid of all the nonsense in our system and took it down to nuts and bolts. Then he made sure that everyone knew how to handle his assignment. We'd study the films and then he'd cook dinner for us. It was different later, after we started winning. Then he became kind of a big shot. He was the toast of the town, and everyone knew he was the brains behind our offense. He handled the Jim Lee Howell thing great, but Howell must have been secretly jealous.

Vince had a good relationship with Wellington Mara, the Giants owner, because Wellington was close to Coach Red Blaik at Army, and Vince was an assistant there before he came to the Giants. Wellington was all football, and he was incredibly loyal to his coaches and players. It took him forever to fire Steve Owen before Howell, and it was the same thing with Allie Sherman after Howell.

Vince and Wellington both were devout Catholics, and they both loved football. So they became very close friends. They would take trips together with their wives. It was obvious to everybody, even Landry, that Vince would be the next head coach of the Giants. But Vince knew that Wellington wouldn't fire Howell, so he took the Green Bay job after we got beat by the Colts in that great '58 championship game.

Only a year later, Howell walked in and resigned. Nobody had a clue. He just walked in to Wellington and said, "I quit." There was a huge campaign to bring Vince back from Green Bay, even though he'd only been there a year. I remember getting a call from Vince and he said, "What in the world happened?" I told him I didn't know, that I was as surprised as anybody.

Vince wanted to take the Giants job. He really did. But it didn't go very far because Commissioner Pete Rozelle said, "No, you have a contract with Green Bay." He wasn't even allowed to negotiate with the Giants. That hurt Vince's feelings as much as anything that ever happened to him. Every year it was in the back of his mind. He quietly resented the hell out of what Jim Lee did, because Jim Lee had waited until Vince was gone before he announced his retirement.

Even when Vince was having all those great years with you guys, everybody knew he really wanted to be with the Giants. He came from New York and he played at Fordham. They were a national power back in the 1930s, when Vince played there, and he was part of that famous line known as "The Seven Blocks of Granite." We used to kid him about that. He'd show us pictures of that line and there he would be, squatted down until his ass was almost hitting the ground.

None of us who were with the Giants was surprised to see Vince and Landry become great head coaches. We knew how good they were. After Vince retired from Green Bay, I saw him once when we went up there to do a documentary for NFL Films. I didn't know it at the time, but he really wanted to get back into coaching. He missed it. So

He got rid of the guys who couldn't win, and then he became one of the guys with the rest of us.

Frank Gifford (No. 16) was a triple threat during his Hall of Fame career with the Giants, able to run, throw, or catch the ball with equal success. Photo courtesy of AP/Wide World Photos.

he took the Redskins job when Edward Bennett Williams offered it to him. He and Williams were about as good of friends as he and Wellington Mara had been.

When Vince got sick, I went to see him in the hospital. It just shattered me to see him like that. I remember we talked, and when I was getting ready to leave, he looked at me and we both had tears in our eyes. I knew I was never going to see him again. He looked at me and he started to say something, and then he said, "Oh, God, Frank, it hurts." And I thought, "Oh, shit." I just felt so awful. I loved the guy. We all did.

Hornung on Gifford: When Lombardi took the Packers job, he quickly noticed that I had the same kind of ability as Frank Gifford, the former Southern Cal star who had been his left halfback with the New York Giants. He mentioned it to a sportswriter. "The more I saw of Hornung in these movies," he said, "the more I figured he was the man. He didn't have Gifford's moves, but he was bigger and could run harder. Actually, he had better running ability than I thought. And I knew he could throw."

I envied Gifford. He played his college ball in Los Angeles, near Hollywood and all those starlets. Then he got to play his pro career in New York, the media capital of the world. He was a good-looking guy, and the women loved him. Long after he retired, he settled down and married an actress who did a popular national TV show with Regis Philbin for many years. I liked to kid him about being Mr. Kathy Lee Gifford.

The Giants had some great teams in the 1950s and early 1960s, but they never could win the big one. Under Jim Lee Howell, and later Allie Sherman, they lost five times in the NFL championship game after winning it in 1956. But because they were from New York, their players got a lot more publicity—and, hence, a lot more endorsement deals—than the guys who played in Baltimore, Cleveland, and, of course, Green Bay.

But Frank wasn't a figment of some sports columnist's imagination. He was the real deal. As a runner, he was shifty and he was tough. Lombardi loved him when he was with the Giants and respected him after he came to Green Bay.

After he retired from football, Frank was a natural to go into TV. He did so well that when Roone Arledge of ABC came up with the concept of *Monday Night Football*, he picked Frank to be the play-by-play man. He was solid, but bland. Of course, that was exactly what Arledge wanted and needed to have in the booth with Dandy Don Meredith and Howard Cosell.

After the first year of *Monday Night Football*, I ran into Arledge at a Kentucky Derby party in Louisville. I asked him point-blank why I didn't get the job that went to Meredith. He told me it was because I was too much like Gifford. We both were known as good-looking playboys, we had played the same position in college and the pros, and we both had played for Lombardi. I'm not sure that I agreed, but at least I understood his thinking.

CHAPTER 4

Sam Huff on Learning from the Legend

I was in New York with you, Paul, when I learned that the Giants had drafted me in the third round. I got the news in a letter from the team. That's the way it was in those days. There was no ESPN around then to make a big deal out of it.

We were a year apart in school, you were a year behind me, but we were in New York because we had been named to some All-American team and they booked us to be on the *Ed Sullivan Show* or the *Jackie Gleason Show*, one of those.

Our hostess was Kim Novak, who then was an up-and-coming actress. Well, I was 17 years old, something like that, and I wasn't even sure what I was doing in New York. So I asked you if we were going out, and you said, "Yeah, I'm taking Kim Novak." I asked you how much money you had, and you said you had $20.

Well, that was 20 more than I had. I mean, that was a lot of money to me. I had a tough time in school. I'd play 60 minutes of football, then go home to Farmington, West Virginia, and deliver groceries to make a little spending money.

I think the first $20 bill I ever saw was when we went to the Sugar Bowl after the 1953 season to play Georgia Tech. We were having a team meal and a booster named Art Lewis said, "I want you to look under your plate." I looked and there was $20. That's all they gave us.

So, anyhow, here we are in New York and you've got $20—you later told me you really had $40—and you were taking Kim Novak out to dinner. Man, that was really impressive to a poor boy from West Virginia.

When I got to the Giants in the fall of 1956, Vince was already there as the offensive coach. Tom Landry was the defensive coach. They didn't call them coordinators. And I quickly found out that Jim Lee Howell didn't know anything about football, so he let Lombardi and Landry run the team.

I wouldn't say that Vince was a nice guy. He did a lot of yelling and screaming. But I'd also say that you could tell he was a great football coach. I'd watch him working with someone like Andy Robustelli or Jim Katcavage, and I'd think, "That goddamn Lombardi is going to be a great head coach somewhere."

Even then, Vince wanted to be the Giants' head coach. Everybody knew that. But it never broke right for him as far as the timing went. It just didn't open up for him when he was available.

I know Vince was frustrated in New York. We had a great defense, but we didn't have the offense to go with it. We had a very slow offense. We never had any speed. Joe Heap was one of our fastest guys, and I could outrun him. Vince just didn't have the talent on his side of the ball that Landry had on his side.

I mean, we had a very solid defense. To start with, there was Emlen Tunnell at strong-side safety. You played with him, too, because Vince conned the Giants into trading him as soon as he took the Packers job.

And there were so many other really good players—Dick Modzelewski, Harland Svare, Cliff Livingston, Jimmy Patton. I mean, we were the number one defensive team in the league, and the defense was built around me. You know, I was the designated hitter. I made a lot of tackles, and the New York media gave me a lot of credit. Chris Schenkel of CBS always said nice things about me, and, of course, I also made the cover of *Time* magazine. That might have caused some jealousy, maybe even among my own teammates.

I didn't go begging to be on the cover of *Time* magazine. I didn't even know it was important. I read *Sports Illustrated*, not *Time* magazine.

I mean, I was drying off after one game, and this guy came up to me and introduced himself as a reporter from *Time* and said they wanted to do a cover story on me. I asked him what it would consist of, and he told me, and then I asked him how much I'd get paid. That's how country I was.

Man, I needed money. I'd never had any money, not where I felt really comfortable. So the guy tells me that I wouldn't get anything except the honor—it is a great honor, even though I didn't realize it at the time—and I told him no, I didn't want to do it. It just wasn't any big deal to me.

The guy couldn't believe it. He said they planned on taking pictures of me and using them to do a portrait that would be on the cover.

In an era of dominant linebackers, New York's Sam Huff (No. 70) was unquestionably one of the very best.

> **I wouldn't say that Vince was a nice guy. He did a lot of yelling and screaming. But I'd also say that you could tell he was a great football coach.**

He kept saying what a big honor it was. So I finally told him I'd make a deal with him; I'd do the story if they gave me the cover portrait when it was done.

He said he couldn't guarantee that so he'd have to call me back. So three days later, he called me and told me I had a deal. I could have the portrait. Well, I did the interview and posed for the pictures.

Then some time went by, and I almost forgot about it until the reporter called me one day and said, "We have a problem." When I asked him what problem, he said, "If the monkey dies, you're off the cover and inside the magazine; but if the monkey lives, you're on the cover." I had to ask him what monkey he was talking about. Turns out it was the one in space, the one the Russians had going around the world in *Sputnik*.

The monkey lived, and that's how I ended up on the cover of *Time* magazine. I've still got the portrait at home.

The publicity the Giants got in those days wasn't because of me, but because our team was in the NFL championship game six times in my eight seasons in New York. If anybody got credit he didn't deserve, it was Jim Lee Howell. He didn't have to do anything, you know? All he had to do was read off the schedule what time the plane left, what time the bus left, things like that. He wasn't much of a coach. He certainly was no Landry or Lombardi.

When you see some guys, you know they're going to be a great athlete just by the way they carry themselves. It was the same with Lombardi. The greatness was always there; he just had to get the right job. Landry never wanted the Giants job. He wanted the Dallas job, and that's exactly what he got in 1960. But Lombardi did want the Giants job. I mean, he *really* wanted it. Hell, he was born in Hell's Kitchen in New York and went to Fordham. He loved New York, and it was obvious he was going to be a great head coach somewhere.

In those days, we used to practice at Bear Mountain Inn, which is about five minutes away from West Point. Lombardi loved that because he loved the army. I'm sure you know he coached there a few years under Red Blaik before he came to the Giants. He was over at West Point a lot when we would go up there.

By 1958, Lombardi was at an age where he felt he couldn't wait any longer to see what the Maras were going to do with Howell. So when he got the offer from Green Bay, he took it. His last game with us was maybe the most famous game we ever played, the 23–17 overtime loss to the Colts in the '58 championship game at Yankee Stadium.

Even when you guys became great and were winning championships and all that, I always wondered if Vince wished he had hung on with the Giants a little longer because in 1960, when Howell resigned after we didn't make the championship game and Landry left for Dallas, Vince would have gotten the job he always wanted.

With Landry gone and Lombardi committed to Green Bay, the Giants replaced Howell with somebody even worse, Allie Sherman. In each of Sherman's first two years, we played you guys in the championship game. In the 1961 title game, I hit Jimmy Taylor so hard that it dented my helmet. The helmet's still in the Hall of Fame, with a big dent in the top of it. The hit almost killed me. Of course, it almost killed him, too.

But Taylor was tough. He was like getting in the ring with a guy who knows boxing. I had a lot of respect for him. But you blocked for him, too, and I'll never forget that. I'll also never forget that you guys belted us, 37–0, in that game to give Lombardi his first title. That had to be sweet for Vince, to beat the Giants like that. In '62, we played a lot better, but you still beat us, 16–7, in the title game.

From what I could tell, Vince didn't change in Green Bay. You changed for Lombardi, but Lombardi was not going to change for you.

The 1963 season turned out to be my last one with the Giants. The Packers struggled because they didn't have you, Paul, because of your one-year suspension for gambling. So we played the Bears for the championship and got beat, 14–10. That made Sherman 0–3 in title games, and the New York media was on him pretty good.

Sherman didn't like the defense he inherited—it was Landry's defense—and he had to blame something, so we became the scapegoats. He just destroyed the whole unit. He got rid of five guys off the defensive unit. Five! It was me, Erich Barnes, Modzelewski, Rosey Grier, and Livingston.

He really pulled the rug out from under me. I mean, I had everything going in New York and was set. I bought a house. I had a job in the off-season with the J.P. Stevens Textile Company at 41st and Broadway. I mean, my kids were all settled in and everything, and I had a summer home in West Virginia.

It was a terrible thing. I never wanted to be traded.

I took an oath right then that I would never stop playing until I got Allie Sherman fired. I used to lie awake at night before a game and dream about making a play right in front of the Giants' bench so I could just nail him…just knock his head off.

Well, after Otto Graham became the Redskins' head coach, I didn't like playing for him much better than I liked playing for Sherman in New York. So I retired before Sherman got fired. But then Edward Bennett Williams, the owner of the Redskins, talked Lombardi into coming out of retirement.

He gave Lombardi a piece of the franchise, I think it was 15 percent, and he should have given him the whole thing. When I was playing for the Giants, they had a good front office with the Mara family from New York. But the Redskins had no front office, and that was one of their problems. One of the first things Lombardi did was talk me into coming out of retirement to be a player-coach for him. God, it was great to be around him again. I was thinking about becoming a head coach, and I wanted to learn from him.

I remember when we were at training camp in Carlisle, Pennsylvania, his first year back. One day I see this old guy walking around and I say, "Coach, who is that?" And he said, "That's Father

Swaydon. I have to go to church every day, and, by God, I'm going to make it convenient." He had Father Swaydon right next door to us so he could go to mass every morning.

> *One of the things I loved about him was that there was no B.S. ... He never wasted a moment.*

We went 7–5–2 in Vince's first and only season with the Redskins, and one of the most satisfying moments was when we beat the Giants, 20–14, at RFK Stadium. But it wasn't as satisfying as the 1966 season, when we ripped Allie Sherman and the Giants 72–41. Our quarterback, Sonny Jurgensen, knew how I felt about Sherman, and he had a career day. I can't really say that I got Sherman fired, because he coached through the 1968 regular season, but Sonny and I sure gave him a big push in that direction with that game. Thanks to Sonny, I finally lived up to the vow I made when I was traded from the Giants in 1964. So Sherman was gone in 1969, but it still felt good to beat the Giants with Lombardi.

I learned a lot from Lombardi that season. One of the things I loved about him was that there was no B.S. You know how it is. A lot of coaches want to impress the owner with how hard they're working, so they talk about spending the night at the stadium and stuff like that. Lombardi was never like that. He never wasted a moment. Every moment was planned out. Maybe he got that from the army.

Anyway, by 9:00 PM or so on the Friday before a game, he would just say to the coaching staff, "All right, hay's in the barn. If they don't have it [the game plan] by now, we haven't got a chance anyway. Let's go to Duke's." And we'd go to Duke Zeibert's, a sports bar right up the street, and we had our own little section where we would eat and drink and enjoy the rest of Friday night.

So that was one side of Lombardi. But he showed another side after we lost. The worst place you could possibly be was the Redskins' locker room after we lost. He never gave much of a pregame talk when he was with the Redskins, but he'd raise hell after the game if we lost.

He loved Sonny Jurgensen from the first time he ever saw him. He got so excited about watching Sonny on film during a coaches' meeting that he shut off the film and said, "I want to tell you something; if we'd had that redhead in Green Bay, they'd have declared us a monopoly."

And then there was Larry Brown. He thought Lombardi was going to cut him because he wasn't getting off the snap as quickly as he should have. One day Lombardi barked at him, "What the hell is the matter with you? Can't you hear?" And that's when Larry told him that he was deaf in one ear. Lombardi said, "Well, by God, we'll take care of that." And he had a radio built into his helmet so he could hear. Lombardi really liked Larry because he was such a hard worker.

The next year Lombardi died of cancer, and it was hard, seeing him go through that. When he got out of Georgetown Hospital before the 1970 season, we were in training camp, getting ready to play Baltimore in the first preseason game. He came to that game—he was very pale—and he gave a speech to the team. It was the last speech he ever gave to the Redskins or any football team. I sure wish I had taped it.

Hornung on Huff: I've always had a lot in common with Sam Huff. We came from neighboring states in the heart of America's coal country—Sam from West Virginia, me from Kentucky—and we both have always loved football and thoroughbred racing.

I look at the years I played for the Green Bay Packers as sort of the "golden age of NFL linebackers." Hell, the Lions had Joe Schmidt, the Bears had Dick Butkus and Bill George, we had Ray Nitschke, and, of course, the Giants had Huff. He was one hitting SOB, I'll tell you that. CBS even did a documentary on him in 1960 that it aptly named *The Violent World of Sam Huff*.

Because he played in New York, the media capital of the world, Sam got more recognition than even Butkus, who was probably the best linebacker ever. But it wasn't hype. Sam deserved every story and interview because he was the real deal.

He graduated from West Virginia in 1955, the year before I played my last season at Notre Dame. He made All-American and was drafted in the third round by the Giants.

Amazingly, Jim Lee Howell, then the Giants head coach, couldn't decide where to play Sam—it was the same experience I had in my first two years at Green Bay before Lombardi arrived—and Huff almost quit to go home and teach. But Lombardi, who was Howell's top offensive assistant (they didn't call them coordinators in those days), talked him into staying.

In the third game of the '56 season, when a Giants starting linebacker was injured, Lombardi talked Howell into giving Sam his chance. It turned out to be a Wally Pipp–Lou Gehrig thing. Once Sam got the chance to play, nobody was going to put him back on the bench.

The '56 Giants won the franchise its first league championship since 1938, beating the crap out of the Bears, 47–7, in the title game.

After failing to make the championship game in 1957, the Giants played in it five times in the ensuing six years but lost every time. We drubbed them, 37–0, in 1961 to win our first title and squeaked past them, 16–7, to repeat in 1962.

Allie Sherman, who replaced Howell in 1961, traded Huff to the Washington Redskins in 1964 as part of a three-player deal. But Sam grew unhappy in Washington after Otto Graham, a real jerk, became the head coach there in 1966.

He retired in 1968 and had every intention of joining me and some other ex-players in the world of radio-TV. But then Lombardi came out of retirement to take the Redskins job in 1969, and one of the first things he did was talk Sam into strapping it on again to play for him.

During Lombardi's season in Washington, Sam was a player-coach. Vince loved Sam. How could a coach not love a linebacker who once hit our Jimmy Taylor so hard that he dented his helmet?

CHAPTER 5

Sonny Jurgensen: For Lombardi, Preparation Was Key

Well before Lombardi came out of retirement to take the Redskins job, I had lunch with Bart Starr one day in Washington, and he told me, "You would really enjoy playing for him. The games are fun. We have such intense preparation during every week that it makes the games fun. You're never surprised on the field."

That really stuck with me because it was so different from what I was going through with the Redskins. We weren't very good then and the games weren't fun for me. I was playing from the seat of my pants (after getting knocked down). So that's the first thing I thought about when I heard that Lombardi had taken the Redskins job.

He called me right away and asked me to come into his office. I went in and sat down. The very first thing Vince said to me was, "You know, I've heard a lot of good things about you and a lot of bad things. I'm sure that you've heard a lot of good and bad things about me. The only thing I ask of you is to be yourself. Don't try to emulate anybody and be something you're not. If you do that, we'll have no problems. Any questions?"

I said, "No sir," and he said, "Well, we're ready to go." So I got up to go and he said, "One more thing: I'm going to be on your ass more than anybody else because you're the leader of this team and if I'm on your ass, everybody else will fall into line."

He didn't say anything about my weight, and I couldn't believe it. Every other coach I'd ever played for was always on me about losing weight. But not Lombardi. He knew I'd be in shape. He knew that if I could go through his practices, I'd be in shape.

None of us were prepared for his practices. You'd do those ups and downs, 75 of 'em, and then he'd say, "Okay, Sonny, take them around the backstop." I couldn't even see the backstop. But you'd go around that, about 100 yards, and come back and then he'd start the agility stuff. It's hot as hell and soon everybody's gasping for air.

But he'd say, "In Green Bay, we had a record. We did so-and-so number of these exercises and we're going to see if we can break that record today. He'd put some guys out in front, and there was this one time we had to pick a lineman. I think his name was Dennis Crane. We were running in place and he just fell forward, just kaput. He was out. And that was the last time we did that.

I remember that Paul Hornung told me about Lombardi time. About how when he calls for a meeting at 10:00 AM, you'd better be there at 9:30. Well, at our first training camp I spread the word, but a kid named Sumpter didn't get it. So he came in at 9:50 and the meeting had already started. Lombardi stopped the meeting and told the kid, "You're holding up 75 people here. We're going to have to start the meeting all over. You must not want to make this football team very badly. You've just told me you're not interested in this job." He got everybody's attention with that.

I'll never forget when we went to Carlisle, Pennsylvania, for our first day of training camp. The excitement of having Vince Lombardi in Washington was tremendous, not only for the players but for all the fans. So this first practice, we had thousands of them around the field trying to get a look at Lombardi.

And Vince is loving it. He's back in coaching and he's all excited and totally organized and ready to go. He gets up on top of that seven-man sled that the linemen use for blocking and he's screaming and hollering. I can hear him now. "Drive it, drive it, drive it." And then he calls me over and I'm thinking, "Oh, shit, he wants me to hit that sled.

Lombardi listens to his defensive coach, Phil Bengston—the man who would succeed him in Green Bay—while defensive end Lionel Aldridge watches the action on the field.

The coach and the golden boy: Lombardi and Hornung trying to see eye-to-eye on the sideline.

The victorious coach receives congratulations after the first win of the Lombardi era in Green Bay.

Lombardi and Hornung leave Lambeau Field victoriously after defeating the Cleveland Browns in the 1965 NFL title game.

Mr. and Mrs. (Marie) Lombardi.

The coach is all smiles (top) despite losing the 1960 title game to the Philadelphia Eagles (Green Bay would claim the title the following year). Behind him is newly appointed NFL commissioner Pete Rozelle. Below, Lombardi beams again, this time after winning Super Bowl I, 35–10, over the Kansas City Chiefs.

The coach with two of the greatest stars of the Lombardi era: overseeing an interview with Bart Starr (top) and on the sideline with Hornung during a break in the action.

Hornung's address wins Lombardi's obvious approval at an event honoring the coach.

But he didn't. He was looking at the crowd outside the chain-link fence and he said, "See those two priests over there?" And I finally saw them and he said, "Go let them in practice." I said, "What?" And he said, "They're my agents." So of all the people watching us, he picked out these two priests.

> *Lombardi taught you how to anticipate and react no matter what the situation. He prepared you, then he let you play.*

Later that same practice, we were running a basic passing play. After the second time, he told me, "You're throwing the ball too quickly." And I said, "You haven't seen our offensive line, have you? I'm used to throwing it quick, Coach." And he said, "You little so-and-so, you do what I tell you to do. Give the play a chance to develop." So I did it three times, and then he turned it over to Gary Beban, my backup quarterback.

Gary had won the Heisman Trophy at UCLA, but that didn't mean anything to Lombardi. So three times Gary went to the wrong side. With that, Lombardi threw his baseball cap at him. He said, "If you can't understand that play, find another position. That's the most basic thing we do. Don't ever get behind the center again." So Beban says to me, "What should I do?" And I said, "Don't ask me—I'm trying to do things right myself." And that was the last time Beban ever played quarterback.

After practice, Lombardi had this special house across the street where he'd meet the media and have a cold beer. He called it his "Five O'Clock Club," and he expected his whole staff to attend. One time our trainer missed it because he was treating players. Well, Lombardi chewed him out. "Everybody is there," he yelled. "Nobody skips the Five O'Clock Club. Do your training before that." He was particular about everything.

I disagree with Henry Jordan's old line about him treating everybody the same—like dogs. That wasn't the case at all. He treated everybody like adults. I really think that when you go back and look at him, he didn't want the best football players. He wanted the most dedicated players, the ones who would give him 100 percent. He wanted people who were going to pay the price. If you gave him 100 percent, he liked that.

He felt that if you gave everything you had, you never really got beat. You just ran out of time. He'd say, "What we were doing was working, and was going to work, but we just didn't have enough bullets."

I think his secret was his ability to teach and communicate. His skills were so much better than anybody else's. He would explain a basic play, tell everybody exactly what they were supposed to do. Then he would leave the room and go watch what the defense was doing and turn it over to Assistant Bill Austin.

So you're impressed with the way he's explained this play, and Austin would draw up the same play, but you'd look at it and say, "This play can't work." Nothing against Austin, but he just didn't have the ability to communicate, to make you believe, the way that Lombardi did.

He didn't really care what the other team did. He only cared about how well we would execute our stuff. We'd play Dallas and he'd say, "They come with all this crazy stuff, these safety blitzes and all that, but we don't care about these things. We don't care about that. You may recognize it [a defense] and you may not, but don't worry about it." And so I didn't. I don't think I forced a ball into coverage the entire season. You threw it to the weakness of the defense, that's what Lombardi taught.

Lombardi taught you how to anticipate and react no matter what the situation. He prepared you; then he let you play. Before our first exhibition game, the reporters gathered around him and one of them asked, "Coach, are you going to call Sonny's plays tomorrow?" And he said, "Let me tell you something. If I haven't been able to convey to

When Lombardi took the Redskins job at the end of his career, he had the opportunity to coach Jurgensen—whose quarterbacking talents he held in the highest regard. Photo courtesy of AP/Wide World Photos.

> **He wanted the most dedicated players, the ones who would give him 100 percent. He wanted people who were going to pay the price.**

him what I want him to do in the game, then they should fire me right now. He knows what to do." He said that to the reporter, and it just about blew my mind.

These coaches today want to choreograph everything. They call the plays and don't give the quarterback an opportunity to think through games the way we did. They're mechanics now. They've made it a coaches' game instead of a players' game. That's too bad. A quarterback in the huddle has a better feel for the game than a coach on the sideline.

I used psychology in the huddle. I'd say to a receiver, "If you can't beat this guy on a slanting pattern, I'm not gonna throw it to you. So tell me. Tell me now." You see, I've put this guy on the spot in front of all the other guys. He's not going to tell me he can't beat the defensive guy, so he's going to bust his tail to do it. Lombardi understood that. He was a players' coach. I think his system would still work in today's game.

Many times I think about the 18 years I played, and, gosh, I wish I'd had him the whole time. Going back to our very first practice, when he said, "You're throwing it too quickly—give that thing time to develop," I understand why Green Bay was so successful, and how much more fun I'd have had if I'd had this man throughout my career.

I mean, you didn't have wasted time at practice. Everybody was moving, and everything was planned to the second. He was so organized and paid so much attention to detail. You did everything in an hour and 40 minutes. You all were lucky to have had him all those years in Green Bay.

He was just a special man. At our training facility, we had this room down underneath the dorm. And he'd come in and have a few beers with us. He'd hang around a long time and then, when he wanted to go to bed, he'd say, "OKAY, you guys can take it from here," and then he'd leave and go upstairs. And we were going, "My God, we've got a tub of beer and we can sit here and have some fun." Which we did.

One game we were behind and we had a first-and-goal at the 4-yard line. And I went on a little play-action and threw a touchdown pass. I figure he's going to be happy about it. Instead, the conversation went like this:

Lombardi: "What are you doing?"

Me: "What did I do wrong? You know, we scored."

Lombardi: "Let me tell you something—don't you ever do that again."

Me: "Why is that? What did I do wrong, Coach?"

Lombardi: "You've got to get everyone on the team involved in scoring a touchdown. We want the line to be happy. We want the backs to be happy. I know you can do that. We want to run the football into the end zone. We don't want you throwing a touchdown. You can't do it on first [down]. You can do it on third down, but don't ever do it on first down again. We want everybody to be involved, not just you and the receiver."

We did a lot of things well under Lombardi, and we had a winning season for the first time in a long time. I completed 60 percent of my passes and had a lot of yards. After the season, I go into the Redskins office, and I walk back to see the coaches. He comes in and then, right in front of all the coaches, he says to me, "You know I appreciate how hard you've worked; you had a helluva year and you didn't even know the system."

And then he got into all this stuff about that next year I'd complete 70 percent of my passes and we were going to have a better year and we were going to win. And he said, "We know now what we have." And I said, "Thank you, Coach, but, you know, you told me that I was going to get the best pass protection I've ever had here, and look how many times I got sacked." He said, "Yeah, but you knew the personnel better than I did." And he walked out laughing. He just laughed and laughed.

Hornung on Jurgensen: Lombardi liked to say that if we'd had Sonny Jurgensen as our quarterback at Green Bay, we would have been invincible. This wasn't a knock on Bart Starr, whom Lombardi loved, as much as it was an acknowledgment that Sonny was one of the best pure drop-back passers in NFL history. Hell, he may have been the best.

But there was more to Sonny than just throwing the football, and I'm not sure Lombardi ever thought that through. I mean, Sonny liked to have a good time about as much as I did. The two of us together may have been too much for even Lombardi to handle.

The media never gave Sonny the credit he deserved because he spent most of his career on some pretty ordinary teams. He played his college ball at Duke, which always is a doormat in the ACC, and he always seemed to be at the wrong place at the wrong time in the NFL.

For example, he was drafted out of college by the Eagles in 1957, but he spent his first four years as Norm Van Brocklin's backup. It was Van Brocklin, not Jurgensen, who took the Eagles to the 1960 NFL championship game, where they beat my Packers team, 17–13.

I kicked two field goals and an extra point in that game, but the Eagles broke a big kickoff return that set up the game-winning TD in the fourth quarter. On the last play of the game, Chuck Bednarik, the "iron man" who played center on offense and linebacker on defense, stopped our Jimmy Taylor at Philadelphia's 10-yard line.

The Eagles traded Sonny to the Redskins in 1964, and that's when Sonny blossomed. For the next 11 seasons, he ran clinics on Sunday afternoon. He could throw long or short, found the seams in defenses, and was as good as Unitas at running the two-minute drill. He made the Pro Bowl five times, won three NFL passing titles, and threw for 32,224 yards.

Lombardi loved him. "He may be the best the league has ever seen," he told me and anybody else who would listen. He is the best I have seen.

CHAPTER 6

Larry Brown: Coach Helped Me to Overcome the Pressure

I never really had any intentions of playing professional football. At Kansas State, we built our offense around Lynn Dickey, who went on to become an NFL quarterback, and I mainly blocked for Mack Herron and Cornelius Green. But one day our coach, Vince Gibson, came up and told me I was going to be drafted in the fifth round. It was quite a surprise to me.

I didn't really think any more about it until one day I got a phone call from a guy who said, "Welcome to the Washington Redskins." I had been drafted, just like Vince said, but in the eighth round, not the fifth. At the time, the Redskins' coach was Otto Graham. They had gone only 5–9 in 1968, so they were not one of the league's better teams.

But sometime after the draft, the news broke that Graham had been fired and that Vince Lombardi was going to coach the team. I had followed football enough to know that he had been extremely successful with Green Bay and that he had coached with the Giants before that. But that's about all I knew, so I started inquiring about him. Everything I heard was pretty intimidating.

I met him at what they called a mini-camp, which was sort of an introductory camp for rookies and newcomers, but I didn't really get to know him until our regular preseason camp. At first, it was very, very tough for me. I worked very, very hard, and I was always trying to impress him with my ability to get the job done. But he would never give me any sign that I was making any progress.

> **He made me so nervous in practice that I couldn't catch it. I'd drop every pass that was thrown to me, and every time I'd drop it, I'd have to run a lap.**

The hardest part was what he considered warming up. He called them "grass drills," and they were brutal. I think he used them primarily for weeding out the guys he wanted to get rid of. He could break you down to the point where you were ready to crumble. But then he'd come over and say something like, "You're a helluva back," and that would bring you back up.

At the beginning of camp, he put me at halfback on the third or fourth string. To play halfback for Lombardi, you had to be able to do three things: run, block, and catch the football. I was fine with the running and blocking, but he made me so nervous in practice that I couldn't catch it. I'd drop every pass that was thrown to me, and every time I'd drop it, I'd have to run a lap. It was very contentious between the two of us.

He also noticed that I was later getting off the ball than the other offensive players. He asked me about it and I made some excuse. He said, "Ooooohhhh-kay," in a way that showed he didn't believe me. And he shouldn't have. The truth was, I had been deaf in my right ear since my early childhood. I don't know how it happened, but I had nerve damage and I couldn't hear.

But I didn't tell anybody, even after I got to college. I don't know why. Maybe I didn't want anybody to treat me differently or feel sorry for me. I don't think it ever hurt me as a football player, and nobody seemed to notice until I got to the Redskins. I couldn't hear the quarterback's count as well as the others, so I was a split second behind breaking off the ball.

The next thing I know, a couple of guys wearing long, white coats showed up in our locker room. They looked like they were from a mental hospital. It turns out they were hearing-aid experts, and Lombardi had asked them to give me a test—without my permission, of course.

So these experts tested me and found out I was deaf in my right ear. Lombardi thought about it a while. He finally called the NFL commissioner, Pete Rozelle, to get permission to have a hearing aid installed in my helmet. Rozelle said okay, so that's what he did. When the helmet finally was ready, Lombardi gave it to me in the locker room, in front of the whole team, and told me to put it on. Then he told me to go to the other side of the room.

"Larry," he bellowed, "can you hear me?"

"Coach," I said, "I've never had any problem hearing you."

Everybody laughed at that. I might have trouble hearing the quarterback's count without a hearing aid, but I never had trouble hearing Lombardi. Nobody did. Anyhow, the helmet really helped me. I could finally hear. Now the only question was whether I could catch the ball.

Lombardi was so exasperated with me that before one of our exhibition games, he told Sonny Jurgensen, our quarterback, to throw me a dozen passes during the game. Sonny did, and I caught every one. Didn't drop a single one. After the game, Lombardi asked me about it.

"Coach," I said, "you put more pressure on me in practice than 80,000 people do during a game."

I sat on the bench during the first half of our first game against New Orleans, but then Vince came up to me and Charley Harraway and put us in. From that day on, I was the starting halfback. He realized I had some ability and gave me the opportunity. I just happened to be at the right place at the right time. From that point on, everything I did in pro football I attributed to him.

His offense was very, very simple, and he didn't give a damn about whether the opponent knew what play we were going to run. He just

> **A lot of coaches can win with enormous talent, but Lombardi had the knack of taking a mediocre player and making him great. He looked for something in a player other than just talent.**

demanded perfect execution on every play. He felt that if you executed, you couldn't be stopped. He drilled that into us over and over.

We had a great quarterback in Jurgensen. Back then, people were saying that Joe Namath had the quickest release in the league, but I thought Sonny was quicker. His arm was strong, too. I've seen him throw the football behind his back longer than some people do naturally. And he was accurate. The ball always was right where it should be.

We had a 7–5–2 record that season, which was a big improvement for the Redskins. Lombardi wouldn't let us lose. Every week he had something new to inspire us, and he was believable. Some of today's coaches try to inspire teams and they're not believable. It comes off as

Larry Brown (being tackled) credits Lombardi for his leap from being an unheralded eighth-round draft pick to shining as a premier NFL halfback. Photo courtesy of AP/Wide World Photos.

hokey or contrived. But Lombardi was believable. He was a great leader. Every time I see the movie *Patton* and the way George C. Scott played the general, it reminds me of Lombardi.

When I heard that he had died, I didn't take it very well at all. I lost a great coach and a great friend. I had gotten to know him and felt I had won him over by working hard. Our team was just beginning to jell and we were all looking forward to the next season. We'll never know how good we might have been.

With Lombardi, deep down, you knew that he could be your worst enemy or your best friend at the same time. He was more of a people person than a lot of coaches. A lot of coaches can win with enormous talent, but Lombardi had the knack of taking a mediocre player and making him great. He looked for something in a player other than just talent.

Looking back, the thing I noticed during the season is that he took a lot of Rolaids. I didn't think much about it at the time. But now I think he knew he was sick and he just didn't tell anybody. Sort of like me not telling anybody that I was deaf in my right ear. I wish his problem could have been fixed as easy as mine was.

Hornung on Brown: Lombardi had a unique ability to judge talent. He didn't care as much about how big or fast a player was as he did about how much character he had and how hard he was willing to work. You look at our teams at Green Bay, for example, and you'll find a lot of guys who were low draft picks. But under Lombardi, they became stars.

When he went to the Redskins, he proved he hadn't lost his touch, and the best example was Larry Brown. Here was a guy who was mainly a blocking back at Kansas State. He wasn't drafted until the eighth round. But Lombardi saw something in him that maybe Larry himself didn't know he had. Lombardi made him into the Redskins' featured running back, and in 1970, only his second year in the league, he was the NFL's leading rusher. Two years later, he again won the rushing title.

CHAPTER 7

Jerry Kramer Ran to Lombardi's Daylight

Vince knew I was doing the book during the '67 season, but he didn't like it a helluva lot. He didn't want there to be anything around that might detract from the game or what he was trying to get done.

Everybody on the team knew what I was doing, though, and I got a lot of ribbing about it. In training camp, I first tried to tape in my room, but that didn't work because my roommate would be over there lying on his bed, laughing and making comments.

So then I went to the john, but guys would come in and flush toilets or throw water over the side of the stall. I finally decided that the only way I could get anything done was to go out to my car and spend about an hour there every night, talking into the tape recorder.

It was a fairly compact recorder, about the size of a book, and I carried it with me everywhere throughout the season. I had it in the locker room and on the bus. I just never knew when I was going to see something good that belonged in the book.

Before the Super Bowl, I thought about taping Vince's pregame speech. I really wanted to give people a feel for the emotions and the tension in the locker room. I thought about it, dismissed it, thought about it, dismissed it.

I didn't make up my mind until the Wednesday before the game. We had a meeting to go over general assignments, and at the end of it, Vince said, "Oh, yeah, one more thing. This might be our last game together." I looked at Bart Starr and said, "What the hell was that about?" But I figured then that he might be thinking about retirement, so I thought, "Hell, I'm going to leave it on."

I kept it very quiet. Nobody knew it at the time, and nobody knew it 30 years later. I didn't think it was anything I'd ever go public with. But I finally told Vince Jr. about it, and he asked me to dig it out and play it for him. I'm glad I kept it. I think it gives people a real sense of what Vince was like in the locker-room environment.

I think the thing that's been missed the most about him was his positive impact on the players. He's usually represented as a mean, demanding, screaming SOB. A lot of coaches think that was his secret, and they try to emulate him. They assume that's what he was like all the time.

But what they don't know is that he was a very, very sensitive man. He could tear you apart, but he also had a knack of saying or doing just the right thing to bring you back up and make you believe you could be a lot better than you really were.

I remember a time when we had a goal-line scrimmage early in training camp. It had to be 90 degrees, and the defense was just busting our ass in the awful heat. One play I missed a block. The next one I jumped offside. He jumped in and just reamed me out. He had me looking down, checking my shoeshine. I felt awful.

After practice, I went to the locker room and I was really thinking about packing it in. I really thought it was time for me to do something else. I had been there quite a while when Vince finally came into the locker room and saw me sitting there. He came over and patted me on the back. Then he tousled my hair. "Son," he said, "don't you know that someday you're going to be the best guard in football?" That really got something started inside me.

At the time, I didn't get what he was doing. But when I looked back years later, I asked myself, "How did you miss that?" He knew exactly what he was doing. Praise means a lot more if you haven't heard it before. He treated each one of us separately and differently, but in a way that didn't piss the rest of the team off.

He could get on you, Paul, and you would kind of laugh it off. But I took it seriously when he got on me. I remember getting so mad at him once that I came within a hair of hitting him in the mouth. I really did.

I busted a couple of ribs in a game at Chicago, but I missed one play, caught my breath, went back in, and

He could tear you apart, but he also had a knack of saying or doing just the right thing to bring you back up and make you believe you could be a lot better than you really were.

played the rest of the game. After the game, our team doctor looked at it and said, "You pulled a muscle." Pulled a muscle, my ass. I knew it was worse than that. The doc was just telling me what he knew Lombardi wanted him to say.

So the next week I'm hurting like an SOB, but I'm out there practicing. By Friday, I'm still hurting, but I'm busting my ass in practice to make a contribution. Well, the *Chicago Tribune* had just come out with a great article about Fuzzy and me, saying we were the best guards in the NFL.

We loved it, but Lombardi didn't like his guards getting that kind of publicity. So we ran a sweep in practice, and the rookie playing in Fuzzy's place doesn't allow the back to clear and they trip over each other. The play is totally messed up. But that's what Lombardi had been waiting for.

He tore up to where we were and said, "Best guards in the NFL, my ass. You're the worst. The worst!" Well, I came up off the pile and started walking back to the huddle, right behind Lombardi. If he had turned around, I was going to hit him in the mouth. I had an inner fight with myself. One voice said, "Jerry, don't do it...you'll be traded...you'll be out of here." But the other voice said, "Hell with it—I'm gonna hit him."

55

> **He treated each one of us separately and differently, but in a way that didn't piss the rest of the team off.**

Trying to make up my mind what to do, I stood there glaring at him. He wouldn't look at me. So Bart calls another play and I walk up to the line and bend over. But Bart calls the snap and I don't take a step. Instead, I walk back to the huddle. Now Lombardi knows exactly where we are, but he still won't look at me.

So I said, "Fuzzy, get in here for me—I'm done." And then I walk maybe 30 yards down the field. Now I'm starting to pout, feeling sorry for myself for getting all this abuse. My ribs are hurting like hell. But at exactly the right moment—I don't know how he did it—Lombardi walked up behind me and messed up my hair and said, "Aw, hell, I wasn't talking to you." Just like that, I was over it.

We go to San Francisco and I play. When we get back to Green Bay, I go to my family doctor and he X-rays my ribs. Of course, they're broken. I've been playing with two broken ribs. So I can't wait to tell Coach. I think I'm going to get an "Attaboy!" or "Great job!" Instead he said, "No shit? They don't hurt any more, do they?" And then he laughed.

When I did the book, there was a line in there where I called him a "short, fat Italian." Dick Schaap and I argued a long time about whether we should leave it in there. Schaap said we should use it because it showed how frustrated I could get with him at times. But I wanted to take it out because I didn't want to give him a book with that in there. In the end, Schaap won and it stayed in.

So the book comes out and I give one to everybody except Coach Lombardi. I mean, I gave one to each of the assistant coaches, but not to him. Finally Marie Lombardi comes up to me and says, "Where's my book?" I was trapped, so I went to the car to get her one.

I tried really hard to think of a good inscription. I mean, I don't want to just write "Best wishes" to the man who has changed my life.

Jerry Kramer (No. 64), who says that Lombardi changed his life, helps carry the coach off the field after the Packers defeated the Oakland Raiders in Super Bowl II.
Photo courtesy of AP/Wide World Photos.

So I think about it and finally I inscribe it, "To Coach Vincent Thomas Lombardi, a man against whom all others will be measured."

I gave it to her, and the next day I ran into her in an elevator in Milwaukee, where we were playing a game.

"Jerry," she said. "I loved the book. It helped me understand."

"What, about football?" I said.

"No," she said. "Him."

He finally sidled up to me one day and said, "Jerry, I liked the book." That was a big relief. He didn't say anything about the "short, fat Italian" crack. But I'm glad I didn't put that locker-room speech in there. He wouldn't have liked that at all.

Hornung on Kramer: For my money, Jerry Kramer and Fuzzy Thurston were the best pair of guards in the NFL. Their blocking was an integral part of the "Green Bay sweep," our signature play. But beyond that, their character and personality had a lot to do with the sense of closeness that Lombardi developed among all the players.

Although offensive guards and centers usually are the most anonymous players on any team, Jerry beat the system by teaming up with Dick Schaap, the great New York sportswriter and huge friend of the Packers, to write *Instant Replay*, a first-person account of the 1967 season that became a national best seller and is now considered to be a classic.

Before Super Bowl II, Jerry sneaked his tape recorder into the locker room and taped what turned out to be Lombardi's last pregame speech as the Green Bay coach. He didn't use it in his book. In fact, he didn't use it at all until he finally let Vince Jr. hear it a few years ago.

In 2005 all of us were surprised when Jerry came out with a CD titled *Inside the Locker Room*. It was a collection of tapes from the '67 season that included Lombardi's last speech. I'm sure he made some money off it. I didn't know whether to be mad or jealous, but I finally picked jealous.

Vince loved Jerry. But I'm also sure there's no way he ever would have agreed to let him tape that speech because he strongly believed in the sanctity of the locker room. With the Packers, what was said in the locker room stayed in the locker room.

CHAPTER 8

Bill Curry: From Boy to Man Because of Lombardi

I played at Georgia Tech under Bobby Dodd, who was about as different from Lombardi as a man could be. Coach Dodd was stately, dig-
nified, and quiet. Oh, he would get mad, but that was maybe once a
year. I thought that was the way it was supposed to be.

With Coach Dodd, if you went to class and stayed out of trouble,
he would be kind to you. He didn't believe in running players off. With
Lombardi, it was constant emotional pressure every day. I could never
forgive him for not being Bobby Dodd. I didn't know it then, but I was
such a baby.

The Packers drafted me after the 1963 season as a future pick, so I
played as a graduate student in '64 and didn't report to Green Bay
until '65. I was a 212-pound center, and I didn't think I had any natural
ability. But here I was with the great Packers. I was terrified. But Paul
Hornung and Willie Davis and some others told me I could handle
Lombardi.

But I also was lucky. Lombardi had just traded Jim Ringo, who had
been his starting center for years, and he wanted to play Bob Skoronski
at tackle. Kenny Bowman was supposed to take over at center, but he
got hurt. So I got the chance to play.

The first week I got there, I pulled a hamstring, so I went to the
training room to get it worked on. I was sitting there while the trainer
was working on my hamstring when Hornung came by and asked
what was wrong. I told him, and he said, "Coach Lombardi doesn't

like hamstrings." I got the message. I got out of the training room in a hurry, and I never went back the two years I was with Green Bay.

What Dodd and Lombardi did, in different ways, was to get the best out of their leadership. At Green Bay, Lombardi had something called the "War Council." That was you, Paul, Willie Davis, Skoronski, and a couple of others. You could go to him and say, "You need to back off, you're driving us crazy," and he would listen to you.

Like many of Lombardi's players, Bill Curry followed his mentor into the coaching ranks and enjoyed a successful career on the sideline, including several years at the helm of the University of Alabama. Photo courtesy of Getty Images.

Lombardi didn't believe in com-
plimenting people for doing what
they were supposed to do. If you did
well, he'd say so. But to get praise,
you had to do something really
extraordinary. It was a matter of

**I'll always be grateful
for Coach Lombardi's
amazing capacity to
forgive a young idiot.**

understanding your men and getting maximum performance, not just
maximum effort, out of them. But I never got comfortable with him, so
I played uptight for him.

After the '66 season, Lombardi put both you and me on the list for
the expansion draft. I know it killed him to put you on there, Paul, but
he knew you couldn't play anymore because of your neck. He didn't
have any second thoughts about me. I was expendable.

The New Orleans Saints took both of us, and they were so excited
about me that they traded me to Baltimore before I could even play a
down for them. This was a real break for me because the Colts were
one of the best teams in the league and Don Shula was the only coach
who was then emphasizing special teams.

He spent hours on the kicking game, more than any coach I'd ever
seen. He wanted me to be the long snapper on punts and to play on the
kickoff team. When he called, I told him, "Coach, I'd crawl to
Baltimore to play for you."

Shula was different from either Dodd or Lombardi. His practices
were twice as hard as either one. At Green Bay, we might have two-a-
day practices in training camp for 10 days. At Baltimore, we'd have
them for six weeks, and I mean full pads, going full speed.

Shula was very stern, but he was approachable. At nights during
training camps, Jim Parker, the great offensive lineman, would get up
and tell these ridiculous stories. Shula would actually laugh. He didn't
say much, but most nights he was actually in a pretty good mood.

My first year with the Colts, I clipped somebody pretty good right
in front of the bench. Shula came on the field and got right in my face,
screaming. I screamed back. I never would have done that with

> **Lombardi didn't believe in complimenting people for doing what they were supposed to do ... to get praise, you had to do something really extraordinary.**

Lombardi. I would have fallen down on the field, maybe, but I would never have screamed at him.

A couple of days later, we were looking at the film and here came the play where I was called for clipping. One of the assistant coaches, John Sandusky, said, "Curry, was that a clip?" I had to admit that it was. "Well," Sandusky said, "the next time we're on national TV, you might think twice before embarrassing the head coach."

I felt like I was about an inch high, so I sought out Coach Shula to apologize to him. He said, "Well, to tell you the truth, I sorta liked you screaming back like that. So don't worry about that. Just don't clip like that again." Coach Shula and Coach Lombardi had vastly different attitudes, but the results they got were pretty much the same.

My second year with the Colts, we rolled through the NFL so easily that we were huge favorites against Joe Namath and the New York Jets in Super Bowl III in Miami. I was really lucky to be able to play with two of the greatest quarterbacks ever, Johnny Unitas with the Colts and Bart Starr with the Packers. Bart and John were the same before a game—really nice guys. But when the game began, they were totally focused on winning. They put on a clinic about how to handle yourself on the field and off it.

The week before the Super Bowl, Bill Wallace of *The New York Times* spent some time with me, asking for a comparison between Don Shula and Lombardi. I was too stupid to keep my mouth shut. I said I preferred Shula's methods. He was tough and hard, but not abrasive, and he didn't annihilate a man's ego or harass him. The headline on the sports page of the *Times* the next day read: Lombardi Not Curry's Dish. Bill wrote pretty much what I said, but it came out sounding more acerbic and critical than I meant it to be.

A year or two later, you and I ran into each other at the Old Absinthe House bar on Bourbon Street in New Orleans. That was the Super Bowl when the Kansas City Chiefs beat the Vikings, and we got into a big argument about what would happen if I ever did run into Lombardi again. You said, "You shouldn't have said those things about the old man." I didn't put much stock in that because I remembered the father-son relationship between the two of you.

But you said, "You're just wrong. He doesn't dislike you or any of the players." I replied that if we happened to meet, he wouldn't have the time of day for me. You were scornful. "If he ran into you right now," you said, "he'd say, 'Bill, it's great to see you, how are you? I'm so glad you're doing well.'" You and I got into a pretty stiff argument that went on for a couple of hours.

Well, it wasn't a month later that I ran into Lombardi at the President's Prayer Breakfast in Washington, and you were absolutely right. Lombardi's reaction was almost verbatim the way you said it would be. I felt ashamed, and I said at the time, "I'd like to visit with you, Coach." He said, "Well, I'd like to see you, too, and visit." It was all very sincere and the first time I'd really felt close to him at all.

This would have been February of 1970, and only a few months later he was stricken with cancer. When that happened, I was in Washington, in the midst of negotiations with the owners of the Colts. Bob Long was in town—he had played for Lombardi with both the Packers and the Redskins—and he came by the hotel one day and said, "You know, Coach Lombardi's at Georgetown Hospital. Let's go see him."

I didn't know if we would be able to get into his room, so I sat down and wrote a long letter about the way things had happened and how I had come to have such great regard for him. We walked into the hospital. Mrs. Lombardi was just sitting outside the elevator when we got off. Sonny Jurgensen was there with her, along with Coach Lombardi's brother. She went in to see if he was resting, but it was okay so we walked in. I was very nervous. Bob and I had gone by the cathedral, where a priest had said a mass for him, and we had little cards signed by the priest, which we gave to Coach.

You're never really prepared for what cancer can do to a man physically. This robust, powerful man, this great presence, had been reduced physically to where he had begun to wither. His right arm was full of needles and tubes, so I took his left hand and his grip was still very firm. I remember the conversation precisely. I said, "Coach, I didn't know if I was going to be able to see you, so I wrote in a letter the things I wanted to say." I guess I was hoping I would not have to say those things directly to him, but then it all just tumbled out.

I said, "Coach, some of the things you've read have been true and some of them are misprints and some of them were taken out of context. But I just want you to know that honestly, without bitterness, looking at the time I spent with you, you've really meant a lot to my life." He gripped my hand. He looked me straight in the eye, and he said, "Bill, you can mean a lot to my life right now if you can pray." With that, I couldn't speak anymore. I just nodded.

I walked out of the room with Mrs. Lombardi. It was all quite tense and I was very choked up. When we got out in the hall, she said, "Yeah, I didn't appreciate that stuff that you said in the papers at all!" I said, "Well, Mrs. Lombardi, I've grown up a lot. I just didn't appreciate the boost or the kick in the butt at the time, and now I do."

I'll always be grateful for Coach Lombardi's amazing capacity to forgive a young idiot. I owe a lot to my Packers experience. When I think about what kind of football player or coach or person I'd have been without my exposure to Coach Lombardi, I realize just how lucky I was, even though I didn't know it at the time.

Hornung on Curry: Billy came to the Packers when we were nearing the end of our run. He was worried sick that he wasn't good enough to make the team, but I kept telling him he was. Sure enough, he played center for us my last two seasons there.

He was a smart guy, a classy guy, and he went on to become a successful college coach at Georgia Tech, his alma mater; Alabama, where he was one of several who couldn't get out of Bear Bryant's long shadow; and Kentucky, where we got to renew our friendship.

I got a lot of heat in 1996 when I spoke at Tim Couch's senior banquet. He was a kid from the Eastern Kentucky mountains who was rated the top high school quarterback in the country. A lot of Kentucky fans were convinced I was trying to recruit him for Notre Dame, but really I was trying to help Curry, my old teammate.

CHAPTER 9

Max McGee and Fuzzy Thurston Relive the Good Old Days

McGee: The first speech he gave us, he grabbed us right by the ass. After he was through we were all looking at each other like, "What have we got here?" We knew we had a different deal going on. And it went up from there. The discipline and the respect he demanded that we have for him and for each other—it just kept getting better.

Thurston: I've got to tell you one story. When I got traded to Green Bay, it took me two days instead of one to get there. I was late. I walked into the locker room and ran into Lombardi. "Who are you?" he said. I told him and all he said was, "You're late—get on the field." I was scared shitless of him.

McGee: It was because of Lombardi that we were all so close. Winning brings you close together, and he taught us how to win. He couldn't lose. He was a great coach. He could have taken an average bunch of guys and won with them.

Thurston: Do you think we were average?

McGee: No, I think he turned fairly good players into great players.

Thurston: Look at Bart Starr. I doubt he would have been anything but a good football player, at best, without Vince.

McGee: Bart was mentally tougher than any SOB you'll ever see. Vince changed everybody's attitude. We couldn't wait to get back into training camp every year because we knew we were going to win another championship.

Thurston: Everything he did was 120 percent.

McGee: I'm not just saying this because of who we were and what we did, but Lombardi secretly would have liked to have been out with Paul and me. I really always felt that. That's why I know to this day that I didn't go into that first Super Bowl because I was the best goddamn guy left. I went in there because Vince trusted me, just like he did Paul.

> **It was because of Lombardi that we were all so close. Winning brings you close together, and he taught us how to win.**

The night before the game, Paul and I were out at our favorite bar in L.A. Paul told me he was going to leave in time to make curfew because he was getting married right after the Super Bowl and he didn't want to stay out all night. But we ran into a couple of girls, and I was using Paul to make them stay because he was the Heisman Trophy winner with all the pretty curly locks—better looking than me—so I told them Mr. Hornung would be right back after bed check.

Well, Vince had told us it would be a $15,000 fine if we missed bed check. That was exactly what the winners would get. To the day he died, the biggest game in the world to Vince Lombardi was the first Super Bowl, because the NFL was his pride and joy and he did not want to be embarrassed by having this upstart league (the AFL) beat him.

But I go back out to meet the girls and stay out all night. When I come back in, Hornung tells me they caught me missing bed check and I was going to get fined $15,000. Blah, blah, blah. Well, I acted like he was full of shit, but he really scared the living crap out of me.

Teamed up with Jerry Kramer on the right side, Fuzzy Thurston will be remembered as half of one of the most dominant offensive guard combinations in league history.
Photo courtesy of Getty Images.

Thurston: I snuck out a couple of times and Lombardi caught me once. After that, I never snuck out again. He made me do rollovers 100 yards, every day.

McGee: Vince wanted to embarrass you in front of all your teammates. He did me, because he knew that hurt me worse than anything. He chewed my ass and fined me and all that shit, right in front of the whole goddamned team.

But Vince also was about as smart as anybody who ever put on a coaching hat. One time before a big game, he told us that if anybody was caught sneaking out before the game it would cost him $5,000. And he looked at me and said, "McGee, let me tell you something—if you find somebody worth $5,000, let me know—I want to go with

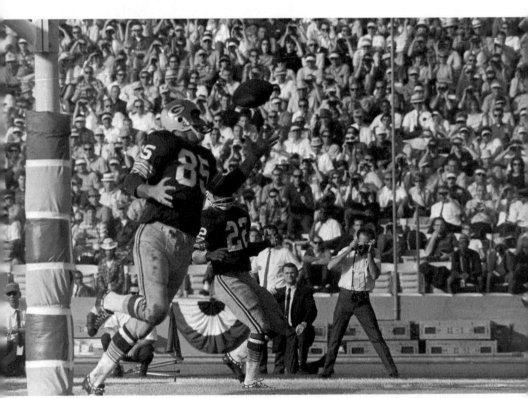

Max McGee makes one of the most memorable catches of his career in Super Bowl I against Kansas City. Photo courtesy of Bettmann/CORBIS.

you." That broke the tension. He could get you so wired before a game that you almost couldn't play. You have to be relaxed. So he knew how to get us to that, too.

Thurston: After that first Super Bowl, Vince and I were at a banquet. We were talking, and he says to me, "Fuzzy, when are you going to announce your retirement?" I was so drunk that I said, "I'd prefer that you let me announce my own retirement, Vince, if you don't mind." He was going to upstage me.

McGee: He wanted to be the big man everywhere he went. I don't really blame him; he deserved it. He got what he wanted, and that was to be known as the greatest coach there ever was in the NFL.

I announced that I was retiring after that first Super Bowl, and Vince came to me and said, "Maxie, I want you to come back next year. If we get a young guy that we're going to keep, I'll guarantee your salary and you can stay on and coach." So the reason I came back is that I was going to be there one way or another, either as a player or a coach. He is going to pay me my contract. Otherwise, I wouldn't have come back.

Thurston: When I finally did decide to retire, I opened the first "Left Guard" restaurant. Max was always our best customer, so my partner, Martini, and I kind of talked him into going in with us.

McGee: I liked the barrooms and I liked steakhouses, so Fuzzy had this little place that I liked. I got in and it was a lot of fun. It reminded me of how we used to like to get away from Green Bay, so we'd find a bar in some little town somewhere. I don't know how many times Paul and I would drive 90 miles an hour to get from some bar to practice on Tuesday morning. We got stopped half the time, so we got to know the policemen. They'd stop us and we'd say, "We've got to make practice." And they'd say, "OKAY, get your ass going." So Fuzzy's place was like those places. The minute you walked into the place, you thought you were in the Packers' locker room.

Thurston: We had a great, great business. People loved us. We were taking in good money, but we also were spending it like crazy.

> **Everything he did was 120 percent.**

You cannot spend it like that. You have to take that money and put it back in the business.

McGee: We took advantage of the popularity of the Packers, and Lombardi liked our business. He felt like part of him is what made us successful. And he was right.

Thurston: It's hard to believe it's been more than 40 years since that first Super Bowl. We've lost so many of our teammates and friends. I was lucky to beat throat cancer a few years ago. And Max, what's your deal with Alzheimer's?

McGee: I couldn't figure out why when I'd tell my wife I'd do something the next day, I'd wake up the next morning and couldn't remember what it was. So I decided to have it checked out. I go to the doctor and I take these tests and he says, "Well, Maxie, you've got the beginnings of Alzheimer's."

Now, I know what that means. I had a brother who went to Notre Dame, Corry McGee. The smartest guy I ever knew. Made straight A's at Notre Dame. He had been a football player and he got the concussions and all that shit you get from playing football. But Alzheimer's finally got him.

So, anyway, the doctors gave me a new drug and it kind of stopped the progression. I still don't have a very good memory. I can remember everything from about 1954 to 1970 as clear as today. I just don't remember what happened yesterday.

Thurston: I went to Lombardi's funeral with former Packers' player Jim Grabowski.

McGee: I remember going to see Lombardi when he was sick, and it was really tough for me. Looking at a guy like that, a guy who had been the strongest guy in my life, I really didn't want to see him that way. I wanted to see him as the guy who was chewing my ass up and making us win championships. You didn't want to look at him, I tell you.

Thurston: It wasn't too hard to cry. That was my first big cry.

McGee: I cry easier now than I ever did.

Hornung on McGee and Thurston: Max and I hit it off right away, probably because we recognized quickly that we were very much alike. He was more than my teammate; he was my partner in crime, my running buddy, my best playmate. And it's still that way, all these years later.

I've never met anybody who liked to have a good time more than Max. I like to say that Max went to Tulane and majored in Bourbon Street. But no matter what he had done the night before, Max always was ready on Sunday afternoon. When he came off the bench to become the MVP in Super Bowl I, he was hungover. But Lombardi loved him, just as he did me. I think he knew that we were having more fun than he was, and it pissed him off.

Fuzzy and Jerry Kramer were as good a pair of offensive guards as any NFL team has ever had. Fuzzy liked to drink and party as much as Max and I did, but he never got the notoriety for it. He stayed below the radar. But when he was in his prime, nobody in the league could outdrink Fuzzy. We offered to put him up against anybody.

After they retired, Fuzzy started a restaurant called The Left Guard, and Max became his partner. After a while, Max went off on his own and got in on the ground floor of the Chi-Chi's chain of Mexican restaurants. Both of them exploited the fame they earned with the Packers into tremendous business careers.

When I was inducted into the Pro Football Hall of Fame in 1986, Fuzzy was there for me, but he had cancer. I was afraid we were going to lose him. But he made a remarkable comeback, and today he's as full of as much piss and vinegar as he ever was. Max was diagnosed with Alzheimer's a few years ago, but he started taking medication and seems to be hanging in there just fine.

CHAPTER 10

David Maraniss: Pride Always Mattered to Lombardi

I was nervous about doing the Lombardi book because I grew up in Wisconsin. All the Packers of the 1960s were my heroes, and I was afraid that if I got to know them and the more reporting I did, I might find out they were a bunch of jerks. It didn't happen. Every one of you guys was great and honest with me, and that made the whole process much more meaningful.

Everybody told me the truth about Lombardi. They loved him and hated him at the same time. They were pretty honest about what life was like in that era and respected the fact that I wasn't out to make him a saint but wanted to write an in-depth book about him. So that made the Lombardi book unforgettable.

It was sort of the same way with the Clinton book. All of Clinton's friends know I wrote the book truthfully and that I wasn't just a right-winger out to get him. I wasn't part of that "conspiracy." I was just trying to write the truth. But, in any case, Lombardi and Clinton. What a pair for me to study. One is the symbol of discipline the old way, and the other is the symbol of baby boomer excesses. But Clinton and Lombardi both had enormous willpower. I think Clinton was the smartest politician I ever encountered.

The reason I wanted to do the Lombardi book was that I had a sense that he was one of those rare coaches who transcended his time and even his sport. But I didn't realize how strongly. I mean, my book sold everywhere. It wasn't just a Wisconsin book.

> **After he retired from coaching and became general manager of the Packers, he was bored to hell. ... He didn't love the owners or the players as much as he loved the game.**

I went to Italy to trace Lombardi's roots. Nobody in Vince's own family had ever done it. My wife and I made our headquarters in Positano, and I would head off into the mountains from there. Lombardi's mother was from a small town, Vietriddi Potenza, in the middle of southern Italy. She was an Izo. So I get to this town, and I had an amazing moment there.

There were two families named Izo, and I tracked them both down. One family threw a big lunch for me. We had all this mozzarella and tomatoes and salami. Then, after lunch, they came out with this sort of family tree, and it had Vince Lombardi on it.

They had followed him from afar, which was kind of cool.

In doing the book, I found out a lot of little things about Lombardi that I didn't know. Of all the people who influenced what Lombardi became as a coach, Col. Red Blaik of Army was probably the most influential, just in terms of organization and what I call "freedom through repetition" and making things simple and clear. Blaik had the same amazing capacity to clarify things that Lombardi had. As teachers and football scholars, those guys were amazing.

Before he came to Green Bay, there was a point when he was going into banking. He had just about given up on coaching because he could not get a head coaching job anywhere. He had signed a contract to work for a bank when Green Bay called. So it was that close.

He had a unique relationship with all his players, but Bart Starr was the perfect quarterback for him. Lombardi took Starr's brain and poured everything he had into it—and it all stuck. That's the way I sort of viewed it after doing my research.

I think the most important game of his career was the first Super Bowl. I mean, he just couldn't lose. The week before the game, he got telegrams from the owners of every other NFL team. In his mind, it would have been so humiliating to lose that game that it would have ruined his whole career. He was under so much pressure, and all of it was self-imposed.

After he retired from coaching and became general manager of the Packers, he was bored to hell. It was the most miserable year of his life. He just couldn't stand it. He just loved the game so much. He didn't love the owners or the players as much as he loved the game.

Although he died in 1970, Lombardi still is a towering figure all over the country and even in different parts of the world. Wherever I

Biographer David Maraniss authored one of the most influential books ever written about Lombardi. Photo courtesy of Getty Images.

> **The reason I wanted to do the Lombardi book was that I had a sense that he was one of those rare coaches who transcended his time and even his sport.**

go, I encounter people who read that book and were influenced by it.

One of the interesting things for me as an author is that after I did the Lombardi book, I wrote a book about Vietnam in the 1960s. Half the book is about a group of soldiers who fought a horrible battle in Vietnam in 1967. I wasn't in the military and I wasn't sure how they would receive me. But then, when they heard I was doing the book, the first guy said, "Are you the guy that wrote that book on Lombardi?" From then on, I was golden with those guys. That's the effect Lombardi has.

At the end of the book, it was fascinating to explore what Lombardi might have done had he lived longer. On the one hand, I almost agreed with Marie, his widow. As much as she didn't want him to die, she thought that maybe he died at the right time because everything culturally was changing around him. You know, the athletes were getting more power, and he would have lost it and he would not have liked a lot of what was going on.

I think he would have adjusted a little more than people gave him credit for. Even in his time, I think he adjusted even more than people thought. Certainly the players of your era didn't have the power they do today, and they weren't as screwed up in a lot of ways. But you guys weren't all saints, either, and he knew how to handle you.

Lombardi was pretty smart psychologically and wanted to figure out ways to win, and he probably would have done it in any culture, at any time.

Hornung on Maraniss: Of all the books and articles I've ever read on Lombardi, the best was the book *When Pride Still Mattered: A Life of Vince Lombardi*. I was one of many people that the author, David Maraniss, interviewed for the book. I wondered how a guy who had never met Lombardi could write anything meaningful about him, but Maraniss turned out to be such a good reporter that he fooled me. The book was very comprehensive, and I read it with great pride.

Maraniss also wrote a couple of books about Bill Clinton that sold a lot of copies. He reminds me a lot of the late Dick Schaap, who spent a lot of time with the Packers during the Lombardi era and ghostwrote *Instant Replay* with Jerry Kramer. He's the type of reporter that really wants to know the truth about his subject instead of just trying to dig up something sensationalistic.

Although almost everyone else in this book either played for Lombardi or knew him as a friend, I wanted to include Maraniss in order to get a different point of view.

CHAPTER 11

Henry Jordan: Lombardi Bred Success in His Players

When I reported to the Packers, Vince asked Jack Vainisi, director of personnel, "Who the hell is this guy?" When he made the deal with Cleveland, he thought he was getting another man who was much bigger than I.

He soon realized how quick I was and decided to capitalize on this. He decided to build his front four with a good rusher at end and at tackle, rather than just at the ends. He picked up Willie Davis from Cleveland where he had been an offensive tackle and put him at left end and myself at right tackle. We were the pass rushers.

Dave Hanner at the other tackle and Bill Quinlan at end played the run. Hanner was a real inspiration to all of us. One hundred percent effort, 100 percent of the time! He came back to playing a short time after an appendectomy.

With this group and later when Lionel Aldridge and Ron Kostelnik replaced Bill and Dave, we got to know each other so well that when any given situation came up we knew exactly what each man would do. Just a look, a nod, or a motion and each man knew his assignment.

Lombardi always paid attention to details. I had been having good success against Karl Rubke of the 49ers; however, before one of our games with them, Vince came to me and said that I should change my tactics, for I had beat him so many times one way that he was probably on to me now.

I would say three of the toughest men I faced were Art Spinney, Johnny Unitas, and Jim Parker, all of the Colts. Art was a great blocker, while Johnny always scared me. He drove you mad trying to figure out what he would do, and you knew that no matter how unorthodox his choice was he would probably make it work.

Jim Parker—well, I spent two years studying films trying to figure out how to beat him. One day we were playing a game and I was trying to play injured. After a play Jim walked over to me and said, "Henry, why don't you get out of here before you get hurt real bad. We play again this year and you'll get another chance at me." He was some player!

Our first division title in 1960 sort of took us by surprise. Suddenly we found ourselves away from our families at Christmas, preparing for this championship game. Something totally new to us! We lost to the Eagles but resolved that this would never happen again.

We won the championship in '61 and *knew* that we were champs. We thought like champs and felt that no one should beat us. Our '62 team was probably the best of all Lombardi's teams; we lost only one game all year.

The next two years we lost to the Bears and then to the Colts. We felt that we were still the best team and did not really lose—only that time ran out on us. We came back to win the next three years in a row.

Vince never got on us after a defeat or a good win, but if we won and looked lousy in doing so then he really let us have it. Of course, during the week we got it no matter what we had done the previous Sunday.

> **Vince never got on us after a defeat or a good win, but if we won and looked lousy in doing so then he really let us have it.**

In Jerry Kramer and Fuzzy Thurston he had the two best guards in the league; yet he wanted them to be better so one day he was on them unmercifully. That night, when we all went out to relax, there were Jerry and Fuzzy in their room studying their playbooks.

Vince knew that Max McGee was good for the team. Max would sit and yawn or wisecrack during his meetings, something none of us

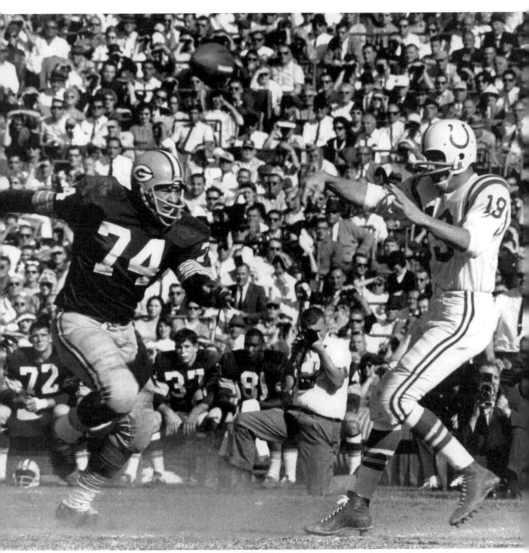

Henry Jordan (No. 74) in pursuit of his self-proclaimed nemesis, Baltimore Colts legend Johnny Unitas. Photo courtesy of AP/Wide World Photos.

> ### *Vince worshipped success.*

would dare to do. But Max got away with it because Vince knew this helped morale.

Lombardi believed in thinking positive. I remember warming up for a game against the Rams at County Stadium in Milwaukee. It was 20 degrees, dull skies, and the field rock hard. The Rams were moaning what a lousy day for a game, but all the Packers were running around saying what a great day it was. Our positive approach!

Vince used to tell us, "You are paid like executives so you will dress like them, act like them, and have their positive approach." Vince worshipped success. He enjoyed being with successful people and learning why they were successful. He wanted all his players to succeed.

Look at fellows like Paul Hornung, Bart Starr, Bob Skoronski, Willie Davis, Max McGee, Fuzzy Thurston, Gary Knafelc, Jerry Kramer, Bob Long, and Ron Kramer. They have all done well since their playing days.

Lombardi was a hard man to get to know. Once we flew together in a small plane and he did not say a word the whole trip. However, when I visited him after he went to Washington, he almost cried upon seeing me.

Hornung on Jordan: Sadly, we've lost some of the guys who played with us on Lombardi's Packers teams. Ray Nitschke, the heart of our defense, passed away far too soon. Emlen Tunnell is gone. And so is Henry Jordan, who Lombardi got from the Cleveland Browns and turned into a Hall of Famer at defensive tackle.

In 11 seasons with the Packers, Henry played on five championship teams and made the All-Pro team five times. He played in four Pro Bowls and was the game's MVP in 1964. From his retirement in 1970 until his death in 1977, Henry was the director of a large Milwaukee festival event called Summerfest. He also did some TV work.

While Herb Adderley and Willie Wood intimidated rival pass receivers with their quickness and aggressiveness, Henry teamed with Willie Davis to give us two of the best pass rushers in the league. Offensive linemen hated to block Henry, a country boy from West Virginia, because he was even quicker than Willie.

I pulled Henry's comments from an article by Stan Grosshandler that appeared in a 1980 edition of a publication called *The Coffin Corner*. It's my way of honoring and remembering the Packers who are no longer with us.

CHAPTER 12

Lee Remmel Recalls
Not an Ounce of
Self-Doubt in Lombardi

Lombardi's first press conference was held in the Crystal Ballroom of the old Northland Hotel in Green Bay. He was totally anonymous nationally when he took the job, so nobody knew what to expect. When somebody asked him what kind of season the Packers would have, he said, "I think you will be proud of this football team because I will be proud of this football team." That was sure different for Green Bay.

Before Vince took the job, the most successful coach in Packers history was Earl "Curly" Lambeau, who was with the franchise as either a player or coach from 1919, the year it was founded, until January 1950, when he resigned under pressure. With the help of such great players as Johnny Blood, Cal Hubbard, and Don Hutson, Lambeau coached the Packers to six NFL championships in the 1930s and early 1940s.

From the time Lambeau left until Lombardi was hired after the 1958 season, the Packers had three head coaches—Gene Ronzani, Lisle Blackbourn, and Scooter McLean—but no winning seasons. Nobody wanted to come to Green Bay because of the losing, the weather, and the smallness of the city. The team had considerable talent in some of those years, but it was just not directed properly.

> **Even after he lost five in a row his first season, I never saw him doubt himself.**

Vince was actually the second choice. The Packers' owners wanted Coach Forest Evashevski of Iowa, who had blocked for Tom Harmon at Michigan, but he said he wasn't interested. So they turned to Lombardi, who was ready to leave the New York Giants because he didn't think Jim Lee Howell would ever retire or get fired by the Mara family. He signed a five-year contract for $40,000 a year—a total of $200,000. I'd have to say it was a good buy for the Packers.

Lombardi was very much like Curly Lambeau in that both had supreme confidence in their ability to win. Otherwise, they weren't much alike. Curly was a big ladies' man, and Vince was just the opposite. During the season, Vince was a terrible interview. If somebody would ask a question he didn't like, he'd say, "What the hell kind of question was that?" His intention was to intimidate the writer, and he did.

In his early years with the Packers, Vince would invite the media to his house for drinks before the season. Then he would take us to the Zuyder Zee or some other supper club before dinner. One year a TV guy told us all about the hunting trip he had taken to the Arctic Circle for his station. Except he'd say "Ar-tic" instead of "Arc-tic," which annoyed me. I'd say, "Goddamn it, Al, it's Arctic."

This began at Lombardi's house and carried on to the supper club. Finally, after very many cocktails, we were still going at it when Vince passed us and said, in his Brooklyn accent, "Lee, it's 'Ah-tic.' Everybody knows that." That showed us he had a sense of humor.

I think Lombardi liked the media a little better than he let on, and I think he respected me as a writer. He never used me to make a point with a player, as far as I knew. Sometimes he was better after a loss than he was after a win because he felt he had to put a good face on a loss for the players.

Despite their teams' on-field rivalry, Lombardi (right) had the utmost respect for the Bears' George Halas.

He had a total commitment to the game and the absolute conviction that he knew how to be a success, year in and year out. He really believed that. I never had any indication that he ever doubted himself. Even after he lost five in a row his first season, I never saw him doubt himself.

He didn't want to lose to anybody, but losing to the Bears was anathema to him. I think the reason was that he had so much respect

> **During the season, Vince was a terrible interview. If somebody would ask a question he didn't like, he'd say, "What the hell kind of question was that?"**

for George Halas, one of the league's founders and the Bears' coach for decades. I remember one game when the Packers beat the Bears. After Lombardi had shaken hands with Halas and was walking off the field, I heard him mutter, "Papa Bear...I love that man!"

My favorite memory of him came after the 1966 NFL championship game in Dallas. We were supposed to fly home for a big party, but the airport was fogged in so we had to check back in to the Holiday Inn in Dallas and have the party there.

We were all standing around in this big ballroom when Vince and Marie walked in. Fuzzy Thurston jumped up on a chair and sang, "He's Got the Whole World in His Hands." It was an electric moment. I think Vince was really touched.

In the fall of 1968, the Wisconsin chapter of the Pro Football Writers Association wanted to get Lombardi to speak at a banquet. Somebody told me, "If you want to get him to your banquet, name an award for him—he loves awards." So we did and he agreed to present it to the first winner. Then I pressed my luck and asked him to say a few words. He said, "Well, I guess I could do that."

Between then and the banquet, in March 1969, Vince left Green Bay and took the Washington Redskins job. I think he was very leery of coming back to Wisconsin because he wasn't sure how he would be received. But when he got up to speak, he received a huge ovation. Then the crowd got so quiet that you could hear a pin drop.

He had them in the palm of his hand.

Hornung on Remmel: Lee Remmel covered us for the *Green Bay Press-Gazette*, so he probably knew Lombardi and the players better than any other writer. We'd see the national guys like Dick Schaap and Howard

Cosell and Tex Maule of *Sports Illustrated* whenever we had a big game coming up, but Lee was there every day at the practices, as well as the games.

We always knew that Lee wanted us to do well, but he wasn't a "homer." He was very professional. When we didn't play well, he would say so. But usually we won, so Lee and the players had a good relationship. When Lee left the paper in 1974, the Packers hired him to work in their media department. To this day, he's the franchise historian and a good friend of the former players.

CHAPTER 13

Jack Koeppler: Singleness of Purpose Made Lombardi Stand Out

I met Lombardi the summer before his second season in Green Bay. It was on the first tee at the Oneida Country Club. Lombardi wanted me to give him some strokes, but I said, "You're bigger than me—let's see how we play today and then we'll talk about it." Well, he thought I played pretty well. The next time we played, he made sure he got strokes. And off we went on what became a very close friendship.

Once I invited him to go deer hunting with a bunch of us up in Michigan. The place we went was pretty desolate at that time, and it was dark as hell. Coach and I got out of our four-wheel vehicle and we had to wade through a small swamp to get to our spot.

When we got there, I held the flashlight while he loaded his gun. He knew about guns from his years at West Point. When he was done, I turned off the flashlight and began moving away. I hadn't gone 75 yards when he yelled, "Hold it...are you goddamn sure you know where I am?" He wasn't about to let me get too far away from him.

He didn't get a deer that trip, but he still had a good time. He loved to play gin rummy, so we played cards all night. Fortunately for the rest of us, he wasn't a very good gin-rummy player. But he loved to be with the guys and have a good time.

> **Talking about coaches, he said, "All of us know an equal amount of Xs and Os. But I have one edge on the rest of 'em: I know more about football players than they do."**

He never talked much football when we were on golf or hunting trips, but he did call Buddy Parker just about every day and talk to him about football. Parker was coaching the Steelers in those days. He also would take calls from other coaches, but the only time I remember him telling us anything profound about football was one night when the TV went out and we didn't feel like playing cards. Talking about coaches, he said, "All of us know an equal amount of Xs and Os. But I have one edge on the rest of 'em: I know more about football players than they do."

You could see that in the way he treated his players. He knew he had to cut Hornung and McGee a little slack, just as he knew that he couldn't yell at Bart Starr. He knew just what every player needed.

I'd say that his singleness of purpose was what made him stand out from anybody else I ever knew.

In the summer of 1961, Lombardi got to play a round with Jack Nicklaus, who was just beginning to challenge Arnold Palmer's dominance on the PGA Tour. Lombardi really wanted to play well in front of Nicklaus, but the day before he got a case of the shanks. I knew what that meant. Sure enough, that night we went to a driving range on Military Avenue until he got it worked out.

The next day's foursome included Nicklaus, Lombardi, Don Hutson, and the pro at the country club. Lombardi played great and shot an 81. When Nicklaus complimented him after the match, he was like a kid with a new toy. That gap-toothed Italian grin really lit up. He was so proud to play well in front of Nicklaus.

When he retired after Super Bowl II, it took him only about two months to realize he had made a mistake. We told him he should go to

Enjoying a good day on the links with budding golf superstar Jack Nicklaus.

> **I'd say that his singleness of purpose was what made him stand out from anybody else I ever knew.**

Phil Bengston, who had been named to replace him, and tell him that he was taking his job back. But he said, "I couldn't do that to Phil," and he didn't.

We tried a lot of things to get his mind off football—took him duck hunting out on the bay and stuff like that—but it wasn't any use. He was restless and nervous. He really missed coaching. So when Edward Bennett Williams offered him the Redskins job, he jumped.

Bennett Williams gave him 15 percent of the team, unheard of for a coach in those days, but the money didn't really matter to Lombardi. He was power-hungry, not money-hungry. The truth be told, Bennett Williams probably could have offered him only a new pair of shoes to wear on the sideline and he would have taken the job.

I came to see him after he got sick. He had three doctors working on him, and one day he asked one of them, "When am I going to coach again?" The doctor told him he wouldn't coach again, and Lombardi said, "Well, I'm not losing my mobility and I've still got my eyesight, so I must be gonna die." The doctor didn't say a word.

I always thought Lombardi got a really bad rap for being harsh and uncaring. He was really a very compassionate guy. After he passed away, we found a bunch of checks that he had made out to former players who were down on their luck.

Hornung on Koeppler: Jack owned an insurance agency in Green Bay, and he became part of Vince's inner circle. He played a lot of golf with Vince and took him on hunting trips. What I knew about Jack, but Lombardi never did, was that Jack loved to bet on the games.

CHAPTER 14

Willie Davis: "Vince Made Me Believe I Could Do Anything"

I played for three Hall of Fame coaches—Eddie Robinson at Grambling, Paul Brown at Cleveland, and Vince Lombardi with Green Bay—and they were all great. But one of the things Coach Lombardi could do better than the others was motivate. He could chew you out one minute, but the next minute he'd say something to make you feel loved and ready to run through a brick wall for him.

I had an offer to play pro ball in Canada coming out of college, but I decided to play for the Browns. The stars of the great Cleveland teams of the early 1950s were either retired or past their prime, which was made painfully clear when the Browns got bombed by Detroit, 59–14, in the 1957 NFL title game. Still, the Browns had the league's best young running back in Jim Brown, and they still had the aura of champions.

Whenever Paul Brown wanted to motivate you, he would say, "If you don't want to play here, I'll send you to Green Bay." It was considered to be a very undesirable place to play, especially for a black. There were no blacks in Green Bay, and the team was as bad as the weather. Who'd want to go to Green Bay?

After the 1959 season, when I found out I'd been traded to Green Bay, I was thinking seriously about seeing if I could still play ball in Canada. But I never made the call because I talked to Lombardi first. He talked to me about a play I had made against the Giants when he was coaching their offense.

> *I still think his ability to analyze and diagnose an opponent was unbelievable. ... It was almost as if he had written the other team's game plan.*

They threw the pitch, and after committing to the inside, I went outside and made the tackle.

Lombardi told me, "I said right then that this guy was an unbelievable talent." He said he told the Giants that someday somebody was going to take that talent and make me use it the right way.

That's all it took. I forgot about Canada and came to Green Bay.

I felt like I was the first black man in Green Bay. I was a novelty. People would tell me all the time that I was the first black man they had ever talked to in person. It was hard to say it was racist. It was just different, that's all. If you were a black man looking for a friend, you had slim pickins in Green Bay.

But race was never a problem on the team, and I give Coach Lombardi and you, Paul, a lot of credit for that. If you had shown any indication of hostility toward the blacks, it would have permeated throughout the ballclub. But you had a great sense of humor, and you always included the black players in your kidding.

Once a reporter asked you about me and you said, "Willie Davis is not only a leader for the black players on this team—he's a leader for all the players." You couldn't have given me a compliment that meant more to me. I truly wanted to be a leader in all the respects by which a leader is measured.

Lombardi did more individual coaching than anybody I've ever seen. He really got to know his players and what made them tick. Once he called me in and he said, "Willie, I know what makes you play the way you do." And then he related my being black and him being Italian and coming up the hard way. He said, "It's very important to me, because of my background, that people recognize me as being a great coach." He knew just how to get me involved.

Hornung and his guards, Jerry Kramer (center) and Fuzzy Thurston, leave the field muddied and victorious after defeating the Cleveland Browns 23–12 for the 1965 title.

Hornung and Jim Taylor (No. 31) get some airtime with CBS's Ray Scott following the 1965 title game.

Max McGee (left) and Hornung consult with New York's Frank Gifford (right) following a game in Green Bay.

Four Hall of Famers in the action on this play during the 1961 title game with the Giants: Forrest Gregg (No. 75), New York's Andy Robustelli (No. 81), Hornung (No. 5), and Bart Starr (No. 15).

On the sideline during the 1966 title game in Dallas, from left to right, are defensive back Doug Hart, backfield coach Red Cochran, quarterback Bart Starr, running back Paul Hornung, and backup quarterback Zeke Bratkowski.

Hornung goes airborne for a score (top), then boots a field goal against the Giants in the 1961 title game.

Hornung eludes the pursuit of Rams Hall of Famer Merlin Olsen (No. 74) during a game in 1966.

From left, Thurston, Hornung, and McGee take the stage to honor their coach on Lombardi Day, following his retirement.

Chicago Bears great Gale Sayers (left) visits with Hornung and Thurston in the Packers locker room following a game in Green Bay.

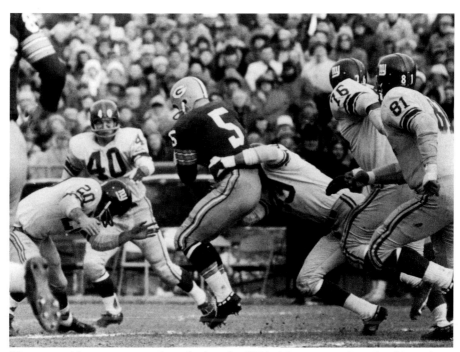

Hornung picks up some yardage during the 1961 title game against the Giants in Green Bay.

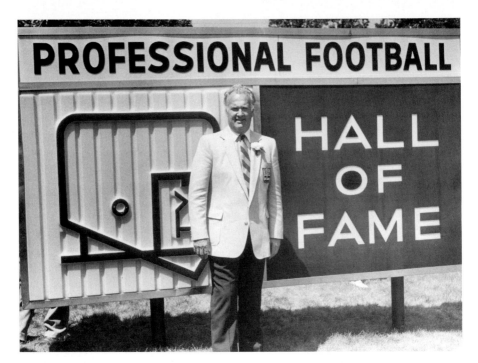

Hornung poses at the Pro Football Hall of Fame (top) and with the rest of the Class of 1986 inductees (below), which included, from left, Ken Houston, Willie Lanier, Fran Tarkenton, and Doak Walker.

Willie Davis came to Green Bay from the Cleveland Browns, and Lombardi helped to mold him into a Hall of Fame defensive end. Photo courtesy of AP/Wide World Photos.

> **I would have gone through hellfire for that man.**

Lombardi had a basic preference for working with the offense. He let Phil Bengston pretty much handle the defense. But we'd see him whenever we'd play bad. We'd tell ourselves on the field, "We'd better get it together or we're going to see Coach Lombardi next week."

Lombardi put purpose behind what you were doing. You knew what you were doing and why, and you didn't want to make a mistake. I still think his ability to analyze and diagnose an opponent was unbelievable. He'd come up to you and say, "You've got to be ready for this or that," and he was always right. It was almost as if he had written the other team's game plan.

Once we were playing somebody who ran a misdirection play, and linebacker Ray Nitschke started chasing the wrong way. Lombardi just went crazy. He knew that Nitschke knew better. Every play, he wanted you to get in a good position and make the play whether it went inside or outside. I could do that. That's one reason he talked so much about my quickness.

He had a pet saying. Whenever somebody would mess up, he'd roar, "What the hell's going on out there?" I think it resonated with everyone. When Lombardi was on the warpath, nobody escaped. Some people had the impression that he never got on me, but he did.

After one game against the Vikings, he had four of us defensive linemen stand up in the locker room after the game and he said, "I want you guys to apologize to your teammates because you didn't show up today." I couldn't wait to play the Vikings again.

He wanted everyone to feel challenged, and it takes a special talent to make you feel that. I was surprised at some of the people we'd trade for. They'd come over as so-so players and all of a sudden they were doing things differently. They did things Lombardi's way because that was the way to win.

In many ways, he challenged me every week. Before a game, he'd say, "When you walk off that field today, I want people to say they've seen the finest defensive end in the league." He made me believe I could do anything.

I was one of the last people to see Lombardi before he died. Had I not known in advance how sick he was, I wouldn't have recognized him. His wife told me that when one of the Redskins players would come by, he would show some kind of appreciation. But when he saw a Packers player, he would just break up.

I would have gone through hellfire for that man.

Hornung on Davis: In two trades with the Browns, Lombardi got a couple of future Hall of Fame players, Willie Davis and Henry Jordan, along with Lew Carpenter, Bobby Freeman, and Bill Quinlan, in exchange for only Bill Howton and A. D. Williams. I don't know how he snookered Paul Brown that badly, but he did.

Willie Davis was a great guy to be around. He was always jivin' in the locker room, so I called him "Doctor Feelgood." He was serious in games, though. He was so quick off the football that offensive tackles had a hard time blocking him. When we won our first championship in 1961, Willie was our defensive captain.

Willie's last three years with the Packers, he roomed on the road with Jerry Kramer. It was probably the first time in NFL history that a black guy and a white guy had roomed together. I don't know if Lombardi had anything to do with it, but he certainly approved. It sent a great message to the team and the rest of the league: there was no room for racism on the Packers.

After he retired from the NFL, Willie went on to a phenomenal business career. At one time he had the largest Schlitz beer distributorship in California, and he still owns five radio stations—three in Milwaukee and two in Los Angeles.

CHAPTER 15

Marv Fleming: The Ring King Sees Lombardi as Coach of Life

I didn't have as much trouble acclimating to the nearly all-white environment in Green Bay as some of the black players who came before me. Playing at Utah, I learned to talk to Caucasians and feel comfortable around them. Whenever I'm asked what it was like to live and play with all those Mormons, my standard line is, "I'm more man, but I'm not a Mormon."

Denver had picked me in the second round of the AFL draft, and I don't think Green Bay picked me up until the 11th round of the NFL draft. So I was thinking seriously about signing with Denver when I got a call from a guy who said he was Vince Lombardi.

"Yeah, right," I said sarcastically. "Come on. Who is this?"

He handed the phone to Bill Austin, one of his assistant coaches, and Austin assured me it was Coach Lombardi. I felt really stupid. He got back on the phone, and, after talking to him, I decided to come to Green Bay. I didn't go there for a tryout. I went there to be a champion, and Lombardi had proved he knew how to build champions.

I came to Green Bay wearing a pair of plaid bell-bottoms that I'd gotten in L.A., and, as you can imagine, that wasn't exactly the uniform of the day on Lombardi's team. I was told frequently that myself and Dave Robinson, who also was a rookie that year, were different from the men of color who had been there previous to us.

But I was young and I was there for only one reason—to play football. So I just had a good time and didn't think about much of anything else. I got along great with Vince. He could adjust. He wasn't made of

> **His attitude was, "I don't care if you're black or white or green—can you block? Can you score?"**

stone or concrete, like many people thought.

I'd like to think that without him, I would have still lived my life by the Lombardi rules. I don't do things half-assed; I do them right. I live up to my words. Still, Lombardi had a great impact on my life. He never gave any indication that he even thought about race. His attitude was, "I don't care if you're black or white or green—can you block? Can you score?"

When I left Green Bay and went to Miami after the '69 season, I brought Lombardi's attitude with me. I remember that somebody picked me up at the airport and took me to the practice field, where Coach Don Shula introduced me to the team. I noticed right away that the black guys all were dressing on one side of the room and the white guys on the other side.

Lombardi never would have allowed that at Green Bay. So I said, "You guys don't mind if I dress right here on the Mason-Dixon Line, do you?" And I dressed right in the middle of the room. The next day, it was the offense on one side and the defense on the other.

I made a lot of white friends at Utah, and before my rookie year, a white girl I knew from school asked if she could come to our training camp and bring her family, who were big Packers fans. They lived in northern Wisconsin. So they came down and met me at the dorm. Nobody was there, which sort of disappointed me. I wanted to run through the halls yelling, "Hey, you guys, I got some white people here!"

We went out and had a very nice dinner. After it was over, her family went back to the hotel and she offered to drive me back to the dorm. I told her to let me out a block away, just so nobody would get the wrong idea. So we parked and were sitting there when all of a sudden I looked up and Jim Ringo was walking by, looking at me.

Ringo was our center and offensive captain, and I didn't know what he would do. I found out the next day when I got a call to come see Lombardi. I didn't know what to expect. But all that happened was that Lombardi said, "Marvin, I know you have a lot of Caucasian friends. Be discreet." And that was it. I couldn't believe that Ringo had reported me. But it didn't matter because he was traded after the '63 season because of a contract dispute with Lombardi.

Lombardi could make you feel so small, but I developed a special relationship with him. He had to go by my locker to get to his office, and he'd always touch me on the shoulder and say, in that Brooklyn accent of his, "Mah-vin!" Even after his tirades, he'd touch me on the shoulder. It was his way of telling me he liked me. When he didn't touch me, I'd get real paranoid and think he didn't like me anymore.

One of the most important things I learned from Lombardi was to always be prepared because you never knew when the opportunity to

Marv Fleming (No. 81), one of the best blocking tight ends of his era, sends Oakland's Bill Laskey (No. 42) to the ground so that Donny Anderson has a path to the end zone in Super Bowl II. Photo courtesy of Bettmann/CORBIS.

> **I didn't go to Green Bay just to wear the green and gold—I wanted to be one of Lombardi's Packers.**

make a big play was going to come. When you hustle, something's going to happen eventually. When I'd see the other guys make big plays, I'd ask myself, "Is it my turn? When's it going to be my turn?"

Sometimes I'd try to make things happen. I'd come back to the huddle and say, "Run the sweep 'cause I can hook [block] my man." You know that famous picture of Fuzzy Thurston and Jerry Kramer pulling to lead the sweep? I think you've got the ball, Paul. Well, I tell them that the reason they're looking downfield is that I've already made one, maybe two, blocks in front of them.

People always ask me about the difference in Lombardi and Shula. Well, Lombardi was a coach of life. Once you play for him, you can leave and go anywhere. Shula was a coach of football. He knew how to produce a good team. But if Lombardi's Packers champions had ever played Shula's Dolphins champions, the Packers would have won.

The difference was Lombardi's singleness of purpose. The Packers were there for one reason and one reason only—to win. He made us develop character as a team. In the last minutes, even if we were behind, I always knew the Packers would find a way to win. With the Dolphins, I never felt that way. With the Packers, everybody wanted to step up because of Lombardi. When he chastised you, you hated it. But when he gave you a pat on the back, you loved it because you craved it so much.

I never really saw Lombardi again after he left Green Bay. But I knew he liked me because I had a cousin, Roy Jefferson, who played for the Redskins. He told me that Lombardi would show the Redskins films of his Packers teams, and sometimes he would say, "I want you guys to block like Fleming," or, "Play like Fleming because he really wanted to play." That made me feel really good.

Looking back, the thing that makes me proudest is to know that I did the job and did it to the fullest every day. I always wanted to finish the job and do it right and do it the best I could. So knowing I did it right is important. But so is knowing that I played with some great guys. I didn't go to Green Bay just to wear the green and gold—I wanted to be one of Lombardi's Packers. If you never wore the green and gold during those days, you don't really know what it's like to be a champion.

To this day, the people in Green Bay love the Packers—win, lose, or tie. In Miami, well, it's more of a tourist town. The demographics are totally different. I was with the perfect team of '72, but we don't have the camaraderie with each other that the Packers of Lombardi's era still have with each other. And not a day goes by that I don't remember something we did or something Lombardi taught me.

Hornung on Fleming: Marv joined the Packers in 1963, and we weren't sure what to make of him. Here was a black guy who had played his college ball at a virtually all-white institution, the University of Utah in Salt Lake City. He was very much his own man, and still is, but he also was a perfect fit for the Packers because he worked hard and had a tremendous desire to win.

Around 1964 or so, when my friend John Y. Brown Jr. was just beginning to turn Kentucky Fried Chicken into the hottest fast-food business in the world, I told my Packers buddies to buy some stock in it. Marv was the only one who listened to me. He invested $8,000, and that turned into $266,000 in only a few months. Marv used it to buy a hotel in Austin, Texas, and that was the beginning of his successful business career.

Marv never ranked in the league's top 20 in any of the statistical categories, but he was one of the best blocking tight ends I ever saw. Vince loved him and so did Don Shula, who got him in a trade with the Packers after the 1969 season.

Marv played in three more Super Bowls with the Dolphins, making him the first man to play in five, and he got two more rings. He and Jim Mandich alternated at tight end on the '72 Dolphins team that went 17–0, the first and only time that an NFL team has gone unbeaten.

CHAPTER 16

George Dixon:
"It Was an Education
Being with Lombardi"

I went into the service right after the start of World War II and became a paratrooper in the 101ˢᵗ Airborne. I jumped in Normandy on D-Day, and I jumped again in Holland, and I was at Bastogne for the Battle of the Bulge. I got shot right through the helmet at Normandy. A goddamn sniper's bullet went right through the helmet, and it rolled around inside and then rolled right down my neck.

Anyhow, I went through a lot in the war. When I got out in 1945, my friend Hugh Devore was the interim coach at Notre Dame because Frank Leahy had taken a leave of absence to be in the service. So I went to Notre Dame because of Hughie, and I loved it. I got to be good friends with Angelo Bertelli, who won the Heisman in 1943 before he went into the Marine Corps, and with Johnny Lujack, who took over for Bertelli as Notre Dame's quarterback. Lujack was absolutely one of the best football players I ever saw.

After I got out of Notre Dame in 1950, I went into coaching. I started out coaching high school football in California. I did that a couple of years and then went to New York University with Hughie Devore. But then NYU gave up football, and that threw our asses out on the street. So I went to Mt. Carmel College in 1953, and Hughie went to the Packers.

At that time, the Packers head coach was a guy named Gene Ronzani, who had replaced Curly Lambeau. Ronzani got fired with a couple of games left in the 1953 season, and some of the assistant coaches—Hughie Devore, Lisle Blackbourn, Scooter McLean—were running the team.

> **Vince was the only coach I ever worked for that came in there and did the goddamn grunt work.**

Hughie asked me to come along with them on a trip to the West Coast to be a sort of scouter in the press box. So that's how I got involved with the Packers and pro football.

I met Lombardi through Hughie. Hughie graduated from Notre Dame in the early 1930s, and then he coached at Fordham, which was Lombardi's alma mater. Lombardi was one of the Seven Blocks of Granite, that great line that Fordham had in the 1930s.

Anyhow, Hughie might have introduced me to him someplace. I didn't know him personally all that well. I'd see him along the way once in a while, and he'd say, "How's Hughie?" or "What do you hear from Hughie?" or something like that.

In 1954, Terry Brennan asked me to come back to Notre Dame to be the quarterbacks coach, and that's where I met you, Paul. I thought you were the most natural big-time player I ever saw. I just thought that everything you did on the football field was better than anybody else could do. You were exceptional. But you also needed to have your ass kicked every now and then.

I remember running into you, Paul, at a coaches' convention in Cincinnati in 1958. We went across the river there to Covington, Kentucky, to shoot some craps or something at one of those places that were wide open in those days. We were sitting there talking, and you said something to me about quitting the pro game because you hadn't had much success your first couple of years.

I told you that you should try it another year because this guy coming in there to coach at Green Bay, Lombardi, was a good friend of Hughie Devore's, who had coached at Notre Dame, and Hughie and a lot of his friends spoke very highly of him. I said, "Give it a chance," and after that, everything went well for you.

After I left Notre Dame, I coached Willie Wood at Southern Cal in 1957, the year after I left Notre Dame, and then I went to the College of the Pacific for three or four years. It was during that time that Jack Vainisi asked me to do some scouting work for the Packers. Lombardi had become the head coach.

They paid $100 to turn in a report on somebody you thought could play for the NFL, so I recommended Willie Wood to them. But instead of drafting him, they signed him as a free agent. I told Vainisi, "You can take that goddamn hundred dollars and forget it. You don't think I know what I'm talking about, screw you." I was pissed because they didn't draft Willie as a defensive back. He was a damn good tackler.

Maybe six or eight weeks later, after training camp started, Vainisi called me. He said, "Geez, Willie Wood is really something. He can jump up and hook his elbow over the crossbar." I said, "For Chrissake, what the hell did I try to tell you?" Of course, Willie went on to become a great player with the Packers and a Hall of Famer.

So maybe that story got to Lombardi, and he figured I must know something about judging talent. Anyhow, he asked me to come help

Lombardi was a guard on Fordham's renowned offensive line, known in the mid-1930s as the Seven Blocks of Granite. Photo courtesy of AP/Wide World Photos.

115

> **The way he looked at things—boy, it was an education being with him.**

him with some scouting and with the offensive backs when he took the Redskins job in '69.

One day in training camp, we were walking to meet with what Vince called his "Five O'Clock Club," the group of coaches and writers who would get together every day after practice. He says to me, "Goddamn it, we don't have any goddamn backs." I said, "Well, you know, we got that one kid, Larry Brown, and I think he's a good one." Vince says, "Oh, shit. You like those tough guys. Give me talent, and I'll make them tough." I can remember him saying that.

Another time, after we broke camp that year, we were staying in some motel right outside of Washington. We had these yellow school buses that would take us to some high school field to practice for a few hours. On this particular day, Vince and I were sitting in the front of the bus together and somehow we started talking about Notre Dame. He said, "I wrote a letter to whomever in hell's in charge up there, and I never even got an answer." He's telling me that he applied for the Notre Dame job—it must have been after they fired Brennan after the '58 season—and they didn't even answer his letter. So then he went to Green Bay.

That's amazing to me. Those SOBs who were running Notre Dame at the time—Father Hesburgh and Father Joyce—have got a chance to get Lombardi, and they're too fucking dumb to know what to do with it. A lot of people just don't understand what coaching is.

There's four fundamental things to coaching, and Lombardi demonstrated this at Green Bay. First of all, the head coach needs to be an outstanding teacher. Second, you've got to be well organized all the time. Third, you have to be a supreme motivator. And fourth, you have to be a very intelligent disciplinarian.

After that one season there in Washington, it must have been in the spring of '70, I was in the projection room one day, just looking at some film, and Vince came in and said, "What the hell are you doing? You ought to be out playing golf." I told him I just wanted to see what some other people were doing around the league. He said, "You did a helluva job with the backs this year, and I want you to know that." I told him I thought my best contribution was silence.

He laughed and said, "Goddamn, I expected you would say something like that." He invited me to go over to Duke Zeibert's with him and have a couple of poppers. We were walking across Connecticut Avenue, I remember it clear as anything, and he said to me, "If you stick with me a couple of years, you can have any job you want in this league."

Vince was the only coach I ever worked for that came in there and did the goddamn grunt work. I'm talking about breaking down the film. I'm talking about every little detail. He came right in there with a yellow pad and a goddamn pencil, and he broke it down. I never had another head coach do that. The way he looked at things—boy, it was an education being with him.

Hornung on Dixon: Lombardi liked different people for different reasons, and you could never figure out why he liked one person and not another. I'm not sure, for example, why he liked George Dixon, my old quarterbacks coach at Notre Dame, but he did. When Lombardi left the Packers organization to take the head job with the Redskins, he asked Dixon to be on his staff.

Dixon was a great guy off the field, but he didn't put up with any crap in practice or in games. Once when I was at Notre Dame, I was caught from behind when I was going for a touchdown. Dixon was furious. "You'll never be caught from behind again," he told me. And to make his point, he made me run wind sprints in practice until I literally dropped. Then he made me get up and do some more.

Come to think of it, maybe it's not so hard to see why Lombardi liked George, after all.

CHAPTER 17

Forrest Gregg on Meeting Expectations and Respecting Lombardi

I came to Green Bay in 1956 but got drafted by the army and missed the '57 season. In those days, the army had a three-month early release program if you had seasonal employment, so I got out in time for the 1958 season. I probably would have been better off staying in the army. We went 1–10–1, and we kinda knew that something was going to happen with our coaching situation.

I went back to Dallas to get a job—we all had to work in the off-season, except for you, Hornung—and one day I heard that Green Bay had fired Scooter McLean and hired Lombardi. I didn't know anything about him, but I thought Tiny Goss, who had played middle guard on our defense when I was at SMU, might. So I asked him when I ran into him at some SMU deal. Tiny never swore. But when I asked him about Lombardi, he said, "He's a real bastard."

Before training camp, John Symank and I drove to Milwaukee from Dallas. We got there three days before we were supposed to report, so we figured we'd spend the night in Milwaukee, just taking it easy. But then John called Dave "Hog" Hanner at camp and asked him how it was going. Hanner had already been to the hospital for dehydration. "You won't believe it," he told John. "He's working our rear ends off."

Well, John and I decided we better get ourselves on up there, so we packed the car, checked out of the hotel, and headed for Green Bay. We got there fairly late, and we told the young boy who was in charge of the dorm that we would probably skip the morning practice and sleep in.

It was "the Lombardi way or the highway."

At 7:00 AM the boy is beating on the door and saying that breakfast was being served and that Coach Lombardi wanted to see us when we got there. So we hauled out of bed and went over to introduce ourselves. Coach Lombardi stood up, and I saw that he was a short guy with a pleasant smile. I figured that maybe he wouldn't be so bad, after all.

After breakfast, we went to practice. We didn't wear pads because, in the past, only the rookies and newcomers had to wear pads. So we did some calisthenics and figured that would be it for the morning. But then Lombardi put us through his famous grass drills. It was about 90 degrees, and it didn't take long before I had my tongue hanging out. I was worn out and I wasn't even in pads!

He never gave us any water during practice, but that didn't bother me. I came from Texas, where it gets pretty hot in August and September. Both in high school and college, I don't ever remember us getting any water at practice. That's just the way it was in those days. When you got dehydrated, the coaches would just call it being out of shape.

I think the thing that sold me on Lombardi was something I saw pretty early in training camp. Under the previous coach, the linemen and linebackers got most of the heat. They pretty much left the quarterbacks, running backs, and receivers alone. But one day I heard some screaming and when I looked over, here was Lombardi, walking right behind Max McGee and barking at him. The more Lombardi barked, the faster Max moved.

And I thought, "Hell, this is all right…I don't mind getting my ass chewed if everybody else is going to get theirs chewed, too."

I was late only once in all the years I played for him. It happened that first camp. After lunch one day, I decided to take a little nap. Next thing I know, Jack Vainisi was on the phone, asking me where I was. Vince was so mad he fined me $10. I was never late again.

Over the years, I've often thought about why I got along so well with Lombardi. I guess it had to do with expectations. I asked myself, "What does Lombardi expect us to do?" The first thing is win. The second thing is for each of us to do our job. You were expected to not make mistakes and to beat the other guy. There was no reason not to do it.

That's the essence of professionalism. If you're going to play, you should want to do the best job you can. And with Lombardi, you wanted to do everything you could to keep your ass from being chewed.

I always felt appreciated by Lombardi, except when it was time to negotiate my contract. He would say, "You know, Forrest, I really can't pay you as much money as you're worth. The quarterbacks, running backs, and receivers make the most money. That's just how the salaries fall." And I never argued with him. Times sure have changed, huh?

I was really very fortunate in my playing career. I played all those years for Lombardi, and then one year for Tom Landry at Dallas before I retired. Both of them came from the same background, having been assistants together under Jim Lee Howell with the Giants, and it's amazing how similar they were in their approach to football.

That one year at Dallas, it was obvious early in the season that we had some dissension on the football team. The coaches knew it, and they would sit down with us and ask us what we thought. When it was my turn, I said, "What I see here that's different from what we were at Green Bay is that it's almost a business to you guys. You might as well carry briefcases. I don't see any real feeling for each other."

And I told them how, at Green Bay, I might be having a bad game and I'd come off the field and say to Willie Davis, our great linebacker, "What am I doing wrong?" And Willie would say, "I don't know, but I'll watch you the next time you're out there." And then he would watch me and give me advice. We really helped each other and cared about each other.

I thought about being a football coach before I left college. After being around Lombardi and Landry, I became convinced that you have to be who you are. If you try to emulate someone, it'll ring false to the players. They can spot a phony 90 miles away. So even though I stressed discipline, I never tried to emulate Lombardi or Landry.

As a coach, I tried to see things both from the coach's point of view and the player's point of view. I never felt Lombardi tried to see things from the player's point of view. There was only one, and that was his. It was "the Lombardi way or the highway."

But he did tell the players what he expected of them, and that's one thing I always tried to do as a coach. If the coach doesn't tell them what to expect, how are they to know what he wants? I'd have to say that most of the players I coached wanted to be the best they could be. They knew that if I asked them to do something, I had a reason for it.

After playing on two Super Bowl teams at Green Bay and one with Dallas, it was a big thrill for me to take the Cincinnati Bengals to Super Bowl XVI in Pontiac, Michigan. To get there, we had to beat San Diego in Cincinnati. It was so cold that day that the game became known as the Freezer Bowl. It reminded me in some ways of the Ice Bowl game in Green Bay in 1967, when we beat the Cowboys on Bart Starr's quarterback sneak behind Jerry Kramer on the last play of the game.

The temperature in Cincinnati was actually colder than it was for the Ice Bowl. But the Ice Bowl was tougher because we played that baby on grass, and the field was frozen so solid that you couldn't get your footing. At Cincinnati, the footing wasn't so bad on the artificial turf and we had heated benches. But we were exposed to more wind in Cincinnati than we were in Green Bay.

I couldn't get warm on the field that day in Green Bay, and my players at Cincinnati told me they couldn't get warm during the Freezer Bowl. I really admire both my teams, the Packers of '67 and the Bengals of '81, for playing as well as they did under the conditions.

As a Super Bowl coach, I tried to draw from my experience under Lombardi and Landry, but I really didn't change anything in our game

Forrest Gregg reached the pinnacle of his own coaching career in 1982, when he took the Cincinnati Bengals to their first Super Bowl. Photo courtesy of AP/Wide World Photos.

> **All I wanted was for him to respect me as much as I respected him.**

preparation. I did notice that the Super Bowl had gotten a lot different from the early ones I'd played in. In the early years, there was one day set aside to deal with the media and the rest of the time you could concentrate on your ballgame. But by 1981 the media pressure was unbelievable. From the time you arrived at the site, it was impossible to get any peace.

After the 1983 season, I left Cincinnati to replace Bart as coach in Green Bay. I had to think hard about it. The fans still had their memories of the great football teams that we had under Lombardi, and they wanted to be successful again. Bart hadn't been able to do the job, so, sure, I had misgivings. But when I thought about Green Bay and the opportunity to put a winning team on the field again, I had to take a shot.

Well, we didn't get the job done, and I was replaced by Lindy Infante after the 1987 season. The whole time I was there, we were essentially an 8–8 football team. If I had to go back and look at that situation again, I'd probably have changed a lot more people than we did. If we had done that, I think we could have had a winning team in Green Bay.

The last time I saw Coach Lombardi was after he took the Washington Redskins job. I was a player-coach with Green Bay at the time. He seemed to be really enjoying himself. He was tickled to be back on the field, and he was enjoying the challenge of building the Redskins. I can't tell you how good that made me feel.

A few years after he died, I was on the staff at San Diego, and we came to Washington to play the Redskins. Marie Lombardi invited my wife and me out to dinner, and then we came back to her house on the Potomac to visit with her some more. She had just gotten the book that Bill Heinz had done with Vince, and she had left it out for me to see, with a page marked. I looked at it. It was the part where Vince said, "Forrest Gregg, quite simply, is the finest player I ever coached."

I was so touched by that statement. I never wanted to be his best buddy. All I wanted was for him to respect me as much as I respected him.

Hornung on Gregg: In his book, Lombardi says that Forrest is the best football player he ever coached. I'd say that's the ultimate compliment. Execution was everything to Lombardi, and Forrest invariably graded out higher than anybody at his position or, for that matter, anybody on the team.

On our team, the offensive linemen got more recognition than they did anywhere else in the league. Everybody knew Jerry Kramer, Fuzzy Thurston, Bob Skoronski, Jim Ringo, and Forrest Gregg. I'm sure Lombardi, who was a member of Fordham's famed "Seven Blocks of Granite" line in the 1930s, had a lot to do with that.

Forrest was very disciplined. I heard Lombardi say once that Forrest would be a great coach someday, and he was right. Gregg took the Cincinnati Bengals to the 1982 Super Bowl, where they lost to the 49ers. Like Bart Starr, he also tried to regain the old magic at Green Bay, but he didn't have as much success as he would have liked.

I thought we had the most intelligent linemen in the league, and Forrest was a big reason for that. He also was smart enough to save his money. I guarantee you he has the first nickel he ever earned. I'm serious. But he was a great teammate and a great guy.

CHAPTER 18

Jim Taylor: "There Was Something Special about Lombardi"

I was Green Bay's number two pick in the 1958 draft, and even though the Packers had won only three games the previous year, I was delighted about it. Unlike some of the players, I liked Green Bay. Coming from Baton Rouge, I liked the small-town atmosphere. We were there to do a job, and football was the only thing on the plate in Green Bay—at least for me.

I spent most of the first 10 games playing on the special-teams unit, but then you, Paul, got injured, and I got to replace you for two straight games on the West Coast. I gained more than 100 yards in both games, and it made me feel pretty good. I thought, "Maybe I can play this game, after all."

But then the Packers fired Scooter McLean and hired Lombardi. I didn't have any particular expectations when I reported to camp. The Packers had other running backs, and I was just determined to earn a spot on the team. It didn't take long to know there was something special about Lombardi. He was a disciplinarian, and, unlike McLean, he kept things simple. I was ready to be led, and I was willing to work very, very hard.

I'm just so happy that I came along in Lombardi's era. He had a lot to do with maxing me out as a player. He used intimidation to push me to the next level, just as he did with a lot of the players. It wasn't easy, but he was exactly what I needed to become as good a player as I could be.

> **I'm just so happy that I came along in Lombardi's era. ... It wasn't easy, but he was exactly what I needed to become as good a player as I could be.**

We always looked forward to playing the Cleveland Browns, and their great running back, Jim Brown. Ray Nitschke and the rest of our defense took great pride in trying to stop Brown, and that's probably the main reason he never seemed to hurt us as much as he did other teams.

Whenever we played the Browns, the media liked to make a big deal of the battle between me and Brown. I never looked at it that way. I was just trying to be the best player I could be for the Packers and do whatever the game plan called for. Oh, I guess we were competing inadvertently, but the reason I wanted to play better than Brown was to help us win, not to achieve some individual honors for myself.

Lombardi loved to beat the Giants, because New York was his hometown and he had been an assistant coach both at West Point and with the Giants before coming to Green Bay. One of our sweetest wins came in the 1962 NFL title game when we beat the Giants, 16–7, on an unbelievably cold and windy day in Yankee Stadium.

The field was frozen and the wind was swirling, and all day Sam Huff, the Giants' middle linebacker, was wearing me out. I mean, he was just pounding me all day. I carried it 31 times but gained only about 85 yards. After one carry early in the game, I was hauling myself up from the ground when Huff said, "Taylor, you stink."

I didn't say anything. But a few plays later, I scored from the 7-yard line to give us a 10–0 lead. From the end zone, I yelled to Huff, "Hey, Sam, how do I smell from here?"

Lombardi liked the way I ran. Whenever I'd get in the secondary and a linebacker or a cornerback approached me, my style was to drop my shoulder so they couldn't go for my legs. Some of the guys said I liked to attack tacklers. Maybe I did. If you know you're going to have a

Jim Taylor (No. 31) was best known for his punishing running style, a trait that was particularly embraced by Lombardi. Photo courtesy of Getty Images.

> **Lombardi believed in the KISS—Keep It Simple, Stupid.**

collision, you had to be ready to take him out before he could take you out.

In the spring of 1966, the NFL and the AFL got into a bidding war over the crop of college seniors that was coming out. The Packers drafted Donny Anderson from Texas Tech and Jim Grabowski from Illinois, and they gave them each a huge signing bonus just to keep them from going to the AFL. I think each of them got around $150,000, maybe more.

I was making $38,500, and I was the leading rusher on the team that had just won its fourth NFL title in six years. I'd been there all that time and had tried to do the best job I could do. Lombardi tried to give me a three- or four-year contract, but I decided to play out my option.

We rolled to a 12–2 record in 1966 and beat Kansas City, 35–10, in the first Super Bowl. I became a free agent, but Hank Stram, the Chiefs coach, and a couple of the others pretty much blackballed me because I was bucking the system. But I didn't care. I took my position and held it and moved on from there.

I finally signed with the Saints but played only a year before retiring. You, Paul, were hurt all year and couldn't play. It was a season where you had players coming from all the teams so it was difficult to get some teamwork, some timing, some tempo. It was tough to play for a bad team after all those great years in Green Bay.

I don't know how we rank among the great NFL dynasties, but I'd say we could compete with any team of any era. Lombardi believed in the KISS—Keep It Simple, Stupid. He worked to make us eliminate mistakes. One of the big things he promoted was total team unity. The offensive side and the defensive side all got along very well.

Coach Lombardi and I had a mutual understanding that it was probably best for me to go with the Saints their first year. Afterward, when he retired as coach of the Packers and was general manager, we had some good laughs and some good camaraderie.

Hornung on Taylor: Jimmy was one of the strongest runners in the league, a guy who would carry it 25 or 30 times a game and just wear out the defense. At LSU, he had gotten into the habit of lifting weights, unusual in those days, and he started us doing it at Green Bay.

He and I complemented each other perfectly in Lombardi's offense. I'd usually run in 10 or 12 times, but I also was a threat to pass or catch the ball as a receiver. I learned how tough Jimmy was early in 1959, Lombardi's first year, when Jimmy spilled some grease on his arm and had to miss a game.

Lombardi put me at fullback in his place, and I carried the ball around 28 times for more than 100 yards. But my body wasn't used to that abuse. After the game, I was so beat up that I checked myself into the hospital and spent the night there. I told Lombardi, "You've got to get Taylor back because I can't take the punishment." But he also missed the next two games, and then we lost three more after he came back, the longest losing streak of Lombardi's era in Green Bay.

Both Jimmy and I left after the 1966 season, but for different reasons. I just couldn't play any more because of my bad neck, so Lombardi put me on the list for the expansion draft and I was picked by the New Orleans Saints.

Jimmy also wound up with the Saints, but for a different reason. He had become a free agent because he was mad at Lombardi and the Packers for giving six-figure bonuses to a couple of college boys, Donny Anderson and Jim Grabowski, to keep them from signing with the AFL.

I didn't blame him. At the time, Jimmy was making less than $40,000 a year and he had been the bread-and-butter running back on all our championship teams.

Afterword by Paul Hornung

In the coach's famous essay "The Habit of Winning," he beautifully stated his thoughts on the subject: "I firmly believe that any man's finest hour, his greatest fulfillment to all he holds dear, is the moment when he has worked his heart out in a good cause and lies exhausted on the field of battle...victorious."

This was Lombardi and what he stood for. It is the most important principle he taught us—to win—not only to win but how to win. Anything other than winning was not acceptable.

Example—I took a lot of pride in the play of Jimmy Taylor. When he had a good day or even a great day rushing, I knew I was part of his success because I was a very good blocker. And so it went on—Jerry Kramer and Fuzzy Thurston took great pride in the sweep and how they led both Jimmy and me to yardage on that play. We were all proud of Bart Starr and how he gutted it out more than once when he was dazed and shook up. He would not quit and would not come out of the game.

Ron Kramer took great pride in his blocking. He was the best at his position. His blocking started the sweep, and he was a bitch. Mike Ditka was the only one who could challenge Ron in the art of blocking.

When we killed the New York Giants 37–0 in 1961, Ron weighed 289 pounds. I received a weekend pass from my army commitment, which was given by President John F. Kennedy. I won the MVP award of that championship, scoring 19 points. Yes, I scored 19 points, but Ron Kramer would have won the MVP if sportswriters had really seen the job Kramer did. I know one thing for sure…Sam Huff would have voted for Ron Kramer, because Kramer kicked his butt!

Lombardi eased up in that game, and I never forgave him for that. I wanted to beat the Giants 70–0. We could have if he had let us finish them off, but he was satisfied with 37–0, especially since he had coached for Wellington Mara. (We never understood why the Giants organization never hired Lombardi as coach. He started out with the Giants and loved New York and all that the NFL stood for in those early years.) But the bottom line was that Lombardi eased up and took his foot off the accelerator. He didn't demand an all-out offensive effort after we had built up a comfortable lead.

That team, our first championship, and the next year's team, which won another championship with a second win over those same Giants at Yankee Stadium, were our best teams in my mind. If I'm not mistaken, there were 12 Hall of Famers on those two teams.

I thought Ray Nitschke was our best player. Butkus had arrived in Chicago, and those two dominated the middle of their respective defenses. What most people don't know is that Nitschke was a former quarterback in high school. Whoever heard of a middle linebacker who could launch a pass 60 yards? But Raymond was an all-around athlete. He was a 7 or 8 handicapper on the golf course, and he was a star on the traveling Green Bay Packers basketball team. They traveled throughout the state of Wisconsin, and Nitschke and Boyd Dowler were the best players.

Lombardi loved Nitschke. He would play hurt, and Lombardi loved it when his players defied pain and played hurt. He got away with murder in some cases. I should not have played or even dressed for my last three games in our first Super Bowl season because my neck was in terrible shape. I had a subluxation of the cervical spine but would have played if Vince had called upon me. Thank God I didn't need to play, and I retired immediately following our first Super Bowl win over a very good football team, the Kansas City Chiefs.

Lombardi was very nervous about the first Super Bowl. He felt we were representing the NFL in the first matchup against that "other league," and he knew that the Kansas City Chiefs were a better football team than the press was giving them credit for. Even though we won handily, we were cautious beforehand not to overlook them or become overconfident. When we beat them, my good friend Hank Stram congratulated me at midfield. I told him not to worry, because his team would be back in the Super Bowl. I was right: they beat Minnesota in Super Bowl IV in New Orleans.

When Lombardi left the Packers, I believe he saw himself as maybe a commissioner of the league at some point in the future. Pete Rozelle was looking to leave, and everyone thought that Lombardi might get the job. But Edward Bennett Williams entered the picture and offered Vince 15 percent ownership of the Washington Redskins and a salary that was to his liking, and Vince missed coaching, so he took the job. It was during a period when perhaps Lombardi was looking over his shoulder and watching Phil Bengston coaching the Packers that I talked to Notre Dame about the possibility of Coach Lombardi becoming the school's head coach. I told the athletics director I'd be willing to call Vince...he would have been a perfect fit for Notre Dame. But they never seemed to be interested.

I thought they were crazy. When you think of all the poor choices Notre Dame has made, not to even give Coach Lombardi a thought, I felt that was stupid. Lombardi had written a letter to Notre Dame years earlier when he was a coach for the Giants, I think, and he never got a response to that either. Lombardi and Notre Dame: that would have been a love affair for the ages.

And speaking of love affairs, I love Green Bay. What a great football town! They sell out every game, and the season-ticket waiting list is the envy of every professional franchise in any sport you care to mention. We even used to play a couple of games in Milwaukee, and that was welcomed by the players in that era.

All in all, looking back at my time as a Packer, I never realized at the time how lucky I was that the Packers picked me as their bonus choice, the first pick of the NFL draft in 1957. The reason, or at least one of the reasons the Packers selected me, was Jack Vainisi, our general manager at the time. He was a Notre Dame man, and of course we got along fine in those early years. Losing—we only won two or three games in our first years—definitely caused the natives to get restless. Vainisi had a hand in selecting Coach Lombardi, and Green Bay will be forever grateful for his decision.

Everything that happened to me in the following years, I give Vince Lombardi all the credit for. He pushed me and many of my teammates to the limit, and it was all worth it.

As I said, this book is my last hurrah. I have been very fortunate to have been a part of writing three books. The first, *Football and the Single Man,* I wrote with Al Silverman of *The New York Times.* We sold two or three chapters to be excerpted in *Look* magazine for $25,000, which was a tremendous amount of money in the early 1960s.

I was single my entire football career, marrying my first wife, Pat, the Wednesday after the first Super Bowl. Pat was from Green Bay, and although I was married to her for about 10 years, we were really only together for about a year—we just never got around to getting a divorce. Then I met my present wife—the love of my life—Angela Cerelli, who was from Philadelphia. Angela was the secretary for Mike McCormack, who was the head coach of the Philadelphia Eagles. We have been together now for more than 30 years, and she has saved my life. I doubt very seriously that I would be here now if I had not listened to her advice on drinking and the need to make some changes in my attitude and outlook during our early years together. I have changed my act completely.

I wrote my second book with Billy Reed, who was at one time a writer for *Sports Illustrated* and who now lives here in Louisville. That book, *Paul Hornung: Golden Boy,* published in 2004 by Simon & Schuster, sold very well, especially in Wisconsin and the Midwest.

We lost Dick Schaap a few years ago. It was Dick's idea to write my second book. Dick was a great friend of the Packers. He had a lot to do with the popularity of both of Jerry Kramer's books, *Instant Replay* and *Distant Replay*. How they have kept Jerry Kramer out of the Hall of Fame is beyond me. It's absolutely ridiculous. Jerry defined the guard position for 10 years. No one was better. Today there are linemen in the Hall of Fame who couldn't hold Jerry's jockstrap, and they know it, too.

Dick wrote the first book about me in the early 1960s, and he also wrote one about Mickey Mantle. Neither Mickey nor I received a penny for either book. My, how things have changed for players today since those early years!

This new book, *Lombardi and Me*, my third and last book, is also written with Billy Reed, and it's one I'm very proud of because it's a lasting tribute to one of the greatest men I ever had the pleasure of knowing.

APPENDIX A

Lombardi's Final Locker Room Speech, Given before Super Bowl II

Boys, there is very little for me to say; whatever I would say would be completely repetitious. This is our 23rd football game, and I don't know of anything else I can tell this team that we have not spoken about a number of times. As it is, there have been trillions and trillions of words about the game as it is. Boys, I can only say this to you. You're a good football team, you are a proud football team, you are the world champions, you are the champions of the National Football League 1967 once more for the third time in the history of the National Football League, only for the first time in the history of the National Football League. No one has ever done that. That's a great thing to be proud of, but let me just say this. All of the glory, everything you had, everything that you won is going to be small in comparison to winning this one. This is a great thing for you. You are the only team maybe in the history of the National Football League that will ever have the opportunity to do it twice. Boys, if I were you I would be so proud of that I would just fill up, I would just get bigger and bigger and bigger, but it's not going to come easy. This is a club that is going to hit you, they are going to try to hit you. You are going to take it out of them, just hit, just run, just block, and just tackle. You do that, and there is no question what the answer is going to be in this ballgame. Keep your poise. Don't let people jumping around out there upset you; just keep your poise. Best of all, there is nothing that they can show you out there that you have not faced a number of times. Right?

Lombardi's Farewell Speech, Given February 26, 1969, in Janesville, Wisconsin

Thank you, thank you, thank you, Bob, for that wonderful introduction. Anytime I hear all of those things, in an introduction like that, I always can hardly wait to hear what I have to say. I am flattered of course to be invited here, to be one of your speakers in the town hall series. This is my first attempt at anything like this; usually I speak at after-dinner banquets, I mean after-dinner speaker at banquets and so forth and so on, but very seldom am I asked to appear in auditoriums, such as this, and in a town hall series.

I want to say, however, that I am flattered to be asked, very much so. The last few weeks, as Bob said a little bit, have been very, very hectic for me. In fact I am somewhere on a cross, somewhere between a Baptist minister who bought a secondhand car and never had the vocabulary to run it and a football...a football coach who died and went to hell, and never noticed the transition.

I have...also I see a lot of young ladies here, in the audience, and I had very little time to...very little opportunities to speak to the young ladies, and when I do, I have to...it brings back a very, very fond memory, or a little story about my little young lady at West Point. She is married now, she is 21 years old, and she has a little…she has a little child, my grandchild, but this happened many years ago, when she was at—we were at West Point coaching, I was coaching at the Military Academy, and Susan, my little daughter, was about four or five years old, and a precocious type of youngster.

Mrs. Lombardi called me at the football office and said she had invited the two chaplains for dinner that evening, and she says you know how Susan is, she said perhaps if you will come home a little bit early tonight, before dinner, and walk Susan around the reservation, and got her good and tired, and we fed her before our guests arrived, she said maybe for once we can have a conversation with our guests, undisturbed.

Well, I did just that, and I did not know who was more tired; I walked that little tyke over hill and dale, all over that reservation, and I did not know who was more tired, she or I, and she could hardly keep her little head up as she had her supper that evening, and we did put her to bed, and our guests arrived, and we had a wonderful conversation during dinner.

And then, after dinner, in those days my upstairs quarters came right down the stairs, came right down into the living room, and we were sitting there having a coffee and a brandy after dinner. And I happened to look up the stairs, and there was Susan coming down, and believe me, her little nightgown was wet, from underneath her armpits right down to the hem of the nightgown.

And I tried to intercept her, but as usual she would have none of me. She gave me a big wide berth, and she went up to those two lovely Reverend Fathers, and she first pointed her stubby little finger under one nose and then under the nose of the other Father, and she said, "Either you or you left the seat up, and I fell in."

You know, I…I did not know what to talk about this evening, and I…I said to myself that surely you did not want me to offer you a John Wayne about the temper of the times, or to speak of peace where there is no peace. And then I discarded all of the major questions of current interests, such as the conflicts of science, with religion and humanity, man falling more and more behind his inventions, the garb and substance of the new ecumenism, the race between population and starvation. The end of missionary zeals and colonialism, the minutes of conversion, guns and the butter of the great society, and I said that if they wanted a subject, someone to speak on the subject in that area, I'm sure they would have invited someone else but Vince Lombardi, not that I am so high on the editorials, or some of our authorities, or some of our writers, who seem to be authorities on everything.

Then I said perhaps a thoughtful discussion on the doctrine of one man, one vote, or the truth of democracy, [or some such subject would be appropriate]. I said [for] any of these subjects, I am sure, they could find many more people, and eminently more qualified, than I am.

And then, by process of logic, or elimination, I came to the only subject, based upon my own experience of trampling grapes in a local vineyard, if that is what you want to call it, mainly football, what it has meant to me as a spectator and as an active participant, the qualities of leadership that I think that are there, and competitiveness that I know is there, and the dedication, all of these things I felt that perhaps you would rather hear.

I want to say that I have been in football all of my life, really, and I do not know whether I am particularly qualified really to do anything else, to be…except to be a part of what I consider a great game.

I think I found, with one year of semiretirement from football, that I had to be an active part of that game again. It is a great game, and I think it is a game of leaders, and I think it is a game which is a symbol of what this country's best attributes are, and that is courage, and stamina, and coordinated efficiency.

And besides, [it is a] Spartan game; I mean by that it takes Spartan-like qualities in order to play it, the Spartan quality of sacrifice, and the

Spartan quality of self-denial, in particular. And it is a game of violent contact, yet because of that violent contact it demands a personal discipline, I think, which is seldom found any other place in this modern world, and it is more than the National Football League, it is more than the American Football League, it is the people who grow up to make that league, it is the Hutsons, and the Thorpes, and the Starrs, and the Giffords, and the hundreds of more like them. And it is the thousands upon thousands upon thousands of high school players who take part in it annually. And it is the thousands upon thousands of college players who take part in it annually.

And it is the millions more, like you and I, who watch it either from the sidelines or on TV.

And regardless of what level it is played upon, it still exemplifies those attributes I mentioned...in addition to that, it has the means and the power to provide a physical and mental relaxation to those of us who watch it.

It was my good fortune, when I was at West Point for so many years, to get to know General MacArthur. Each Monday evening I would be asked by Red Blaik to take the pictures of Saturday's game down to the Waldorf Towers, to show the good general the pictures of the last West Point game.

And he said many things—I got to know him quite well in the course of a year—and he said many, many things to me, and I won't attempt to remember everything that he said.

But some of the things that he did say in speaking about competitive sports, football in particular, he said it keeps alive a spirit of vitality, and enterprise. He was not just talking about the participants now; he was talking about everybody who was interested in the game.

He said it teaches the strong to know when they are weak, and the brave to face themselves when they are afraid, to be proud, and to be unbending in defeat, yet humble and gentle in victory, and to master ourselves before we attempt to master others, to learn to laugh yet never forget how to weep, and it gives a predominance of courage over timidity.

I think those were great words from a great American, and there are other lessons, too, I think. For example, I do not know of another game which in its early season requires the exhaustive hard work, to the point of drudgery really, that the game of football requires. It is a game of team action, where the only reward that an individual gets is the total satisfaction that he is a part of the successful whole, or the satisfaction that he gets from being a part of the successful whole.

It is a game which gives 100 percent elation, it is a game which gives 100 percent fun, it is a game which is 100 percent laughter when you win, and yet it extracts, and demands really, a 100 percent resolution, a 100 percent determination, when you lose. It is a game of quick decisions; it is a game of strategy. It is a game which requires each man that is a part of it to give something, to give something to the spirit of the team, because it is this very spirit that takes 11 hardened and talented men and binds them into a cohesive force.

In this, I think it is a great deal like life, in that it demands that a man's personal commitment must be to excellence, and must be to victory, even though you know that ultimate victory can never be completely won, yet that victory must be wooed, and it must be pursued with all of one's might.

And each week is a new encounter, each year there is a new challenge, yet all of the display, all of the rings, and all of the running, and all of the color, and all of the glamour, and all of the excitement, these things linger only in the memory, but the spirit, the will to excel, the will to win, these are the things that endure.

And really, these are the qualities that are larger and so much more important than any of the events that occasion, just as the flow of all of our daily efforts add up to something which is greater, and certainly more enduring, if they create in each one of us a person who grows, a person who understands, one who really lives, one who prevails for a larger and more meaningful victory, not only now, but hopefully [for] an eternity.

Indeed I think that a quality of life is this full measure of a man's personal commitment to excellence and to victory, whether it be to football, whether it be in business, or whether it be in government, and I think there is a great need in this country for this type of quality leadership in business, in politics, and in government.

And I think, too, it is like life; it teaches that work, and sacrifice, and perseverance, and competitive drive, and selflessness, and a respect for authority is the price that each and every one of us must pay to achieve any goal that is worthwhile.

I want to say this: I think that right now, at no other time in our history, is an age for heroes…I do not think the prizes and the perils, at one and the same time have been so great. A man must decide— and when I speak about man, I speak about you and I—you and I must decide whether we want to provide a full life for humanity or destroy ourselves with our own problems.

And the test of this century is going to be, I think, where the man mistakes the growth of wealth and power with the growth of spirit and character, or like some irresponsible infant playing with danger-ous toys or with matches destroys the very house he may have inherited.

So I think it becomes your obligation to see that we are awak-ened to this need. And also, I might say, a need to develop once again a strong spirit of competitive interests, and I think we failed miserably in our obligation, unless we preserve what has always been an American zeal, and that is to be first, regardless of what we do, and to win, and to win, and to win.

You know, we speak about freedom, all of us do, we see it in the papers. All over the campuses it is freedom of speech, and freedom of this, it is the right to dissent, and all of these things, but I am afraid that sometimes, it is my opinion, that we confuse freedom with license. I think before any one of us can embrace freedom, we must first embrace those things which underline freedom, and I am speaking about duty, I am speaking of respect for authority, and I am speaking of a development of a strong mental discipline.

These are the things that must first be embraced before we can embrace freedom. And I am sure [that] you, like I [am] at times, must be completely shocked by what seems to be a complete breakdown of law and order, and of the moral code. It is almost beyond belief, and it is an unhappy thought, that our youth, the most gifted segment of our population, the inheritors of all of our scientific advances and freedoms, the beneficiaries of all of their elders' sacrifices and achievements, this small segment of the youth—not all of the youth, but a very small segment of youth—seems to have a complete disregard for the indispensibility of law and authority to their enjoyment and the fullness of life.

And then they are joined with a certain group of their elders, who we think should know better, to seek a new right. I am still puzzled as to what that right is, but it seems to be a right to violate the laws of impunity, and the prevailing sentiment seems to be if you do not like the rule, break it.

All of us here, at one time or other, have struggled as individuals, have struggled to liberate ourselves from what you... [refer to as] traditions, and creeds; therefore, I think, as of necessity, freedom was idealized against autumn, the new was idealized against the old, genius idealized against discipline, everything was done to strengthen the rights of the individual, and at the same time weaken the rights of the church, weaken the rights of the state, and weaken the rights of all authority, and maybe that battle was too well won by all of us.

Maybe we have too much freedom. At the same time, it has always been the function of youth to defend liberty, and to defend innovation, and to fight for innovation. And it has always been the function of the old to defend all of their tradition. I do not think any one of us regret the rebellion, but we have so long ridiculed authority, and the family, and discipline and education, and law and the state, that all of the freedom we fought so hard for has brought us close to chaos.

And I think it could be that the people who would lead us no longer understand the difference between themselves and the people, that while most shout to be independent, at the same time they wish to be dependent.

And where most shout to assert themselves, at the same time they wish to be told what to do.

I want to talk about this phase of it, about the leadership phase of it, the quality leadership.

And when we speak about leadership, we are speaking about a position of command, and the doctrine of command can be summed up in one word, the doctrine of command can be summed up in the word *leadership*, and leadership is defined as the ability to direct people, but more important to have that direction accepted.

Now I think you and I both know that that is much too simple a definition for what is a very complex subject.

I think most…of us possess a leadership ability, but unfortunately, leadership rests not upon ability and not upon capacity; having the ability and having the capacity is not enough; leadership is based on a willingness to use it.

And if it is used, it is then based upon truth, and upon character, and there must be truth in its purpose, and willpower in its character. Leadership rests not only upon ability, and not only upon capacity, but it also rests upon commitments, it rests upon loyalty, it rests upon pride, and it rests upon followers.

The educated man is the natural leader, but not all educated men are leaders. Going to college helps, but really a man can receive his inspiration from any place—he can receive his inspiration from the Fulton Fish Market, if he so desires.

And if a man studies his past, and if he studies his country, and if he studies his ancestors, and if he studies the lessons of history, believe me, he is educated.

I think you will agree, we need not just engineers and scientists, but rather people who will keep their heads in this type of emergency, in other words, leaders who will meet problems, intricate problems, with wisdom and with courage.

Leaders, leadership is based not upon one quality, but a blend of many, and…each one who leads must develop their own particular combination, according to their own personality. Leaders, contrary to the opinion of many, are not born, they are made, and they are made just like everything else is made—by an effort and a price that we all pay to achieve any goal.

None of us really are born equal, in spite of what we may say, but rather unequal.

But at the same time the talented are no more responsible for their birthright than the underprivileged are, but the measure of each should be what each does in a specific situation.

And I want to say that has become increasingly difficult, to be tolerant of a society which seems to have sympathy *only*, and I emphasize that word, seems to have sympathy *only* for the misfit, for the maladjusted, for the criminal, and for the loser. Help them, have sympathy for them, yes, but I think it is also time to stand up and to cheer for, and to pat on the back, and to help those who do things, those who achieve things, those who recognize problems and do something about them, one who looks for something extra to do for his country, the winner and the leader.

I want to say, too, that I think above everything else, a man who would lead must be honest with himself, he must realize that he is just like everybody else, he must know that he is just like everyone else, he must identify himself with the group, he must back up that group even at the risk sometimes of displeasing some of his superiors. He must believe that the group wants from him a sense of approval, and I think if this feeling prevailed, I think you will find that production, and discipline, and morale will be high.

In return, if you will give this cooperation, you can demand the cooperation to promote the goals of your team, of your school, of your country, of your business, whatever. You've got to believe in teamwork through participation.

As a result, the contacts have to be rather close and informal at times. You have to be sensitive to the emotional needs of others [and], in return, the attitude toward the leader will be one of confidence, or should be one of confidence, and at times possibly of affection, although that is not the important thing.

But in spite of what I said about closeness and informality, the leader can never really close the gap between himself and the people he does lead. If he does, he is no longer what he must be.

I would like to refer to it as a tightrope that he must walk, between the consent that he must win and the control that he must exert. I think it is important to realize, too, that a man who would lead does not exist in the abstract, but rather is judged in terms of what he does and the specific situation; or another way of putting it, he is judged in the terms of what others do to obtain the results that he has placed there to get.

And the most important element in the character makeup of a leader, and one of the most difficult to explain, is the one of mental toughness, and...mental toughness is many things. Mental toughness is humility, because I think it is important to remember that simplicity is the sign of greatness and weakness is the sign of strength.

Mental toughness, with its qualities of sacrifice and self-denial, and with the other qualities of Spartanism, of dedication, and fearlessness, and love. I'm not speaking of a love that a man may have for his wife, or a wife for a husband, the love I am speaking of is loyalty, which is the greatest of love. The love I speak of is team-work; the love I speak of is the respect that one man has for the dignity of another man.

The love I am not speaking of is the attraction. You show me a man who belittles another, and I will show you a man who will never lead. You show me a man who is not charitable, and I will show you a man who will never lead. I'm not advocating that love is the answer to everything; neither am I speaking of a love which forces everyone else to love everybody else.

[I am not saying], for example, that you must love the white man because he is white, you must love the black man because he is black, you must love the poor man because he is poor, or your enemy because he is your enemy, but rather of a love of one human for another human, who just happens to be white or black, rich or poor, enemy or friend. Hard power is the strength of the school, hard power is the strength of any government, hard power is the strength of the Packers, hard power is the strength of America, and hate power is the weakness of the world.

Mental toughness is also the perfectly disciplined will, and the strength in the group is in the will of the men who will lead it, and the will is the character and the action, and the great hope of society is the character in action.

We are never going to create a good society, much less a great one, until we recognize this, and until we recognize individual excellence once more, until individual excellence is once more. Mental toughness is also the perfectly disciplined will, and the strength of the group is in the will of the men who will lead it, and the will is the character in action, and the great hope of society is the character in action.

We are never going to create a good society, much less a great one, until we recognize this, and until we also recognize individual excellence once more, until individual excellence is once more respected and encouraged. If we would create something we must be something. Character is the direct result of doing, character is the direct result of mental attitude, and you cannot copy someone else's particular character qualifications, but must develop your own particular qualifications according to your own personality.

And when all is said and done, I think a leader must exercise an effective influence upon the people that he leads, and the degree he accomplishes this depends upon the personality of the man.

The incandescence of which he is capable, the flame that burns in him, the magnetism which flows [from] the hearts of the other men to him, no leader, regardless of how great he may be, can long continue to lead unless he wins battles, because the battle decides all. How you do this, I think, is essential to understand that battles are won primarily in the hearts of men. Men respond to leadership in the most remarkable way; once you have won their hearts, they will follow you anywhere.

Leadership is then based upon a spiritual quality, a power to inspire others, sometimes for good, sometimes for evil, sometimes [for] one's own personal ends, sometimes partially evil, or all evil. Leadership that is evil, while it may temporarily succeed, always carries within itself the seeds of its own destruction. I realize that this is a very short explanation of a very, very complex subject, and I want to say, too, that it is a very dogmatic one, but let me say this please, that the difference between a group and the man who would lead it is not a lack of strength, not a lack of knowledge, but rather a lack of will, and the character rather than education is man's greatest need and man's greatest safeguard, because the character is higher than the intellect.

And the true difference between them is in energy. That is true, it is in the strong will, it is in the subtle purpose, it is in the invincible determination, but the new leadership—the new leadership, young men and young ladies—is in sacrifice, it is in self-denial, it is in love, it is in loyalty, it is in fearlessness, in humility, it is in the perfectly disciplined will.

This is not only the new leadership, this is the distinction between great and little men. Thank you.

APPENDIX C

The Greatest Players of My Era

As I was putting the final touches on this book in late April 2006, I turned on the TV to watch the NFL draft from Radio City Music Hall in New York. Coincidentally, it was the 50th anniversary of my selection as the first overall pick in the NFL draft of 1956 and also the 50th anniversary of my winning the Heisman Trophy.

There are a few slight differences between those days and today in the world of sports. When I was selected first 50 years ago (called the "bonus pick" at that time), I signed a contract for $15,000 plus a $3,500 signing bonus. The first pick in the 2006 draft got $46 million, with about $27 million of it guaranteed. But I was thrilled with my selection, and also with my contract and the signing bonus. How things have changed! And to think that the Packers could have selected Jim Brown, whom I consider to be the best football player ever. Period.

When I won in 1956, the Heisman voting was the closest ever up to that point, and I edged out Johnny Majors of Tennessee by a slight margin. I've always felt that since I finished fifth in the Heisman voting as a junior, it helped me win the following year. Johnny Majors was my guest at the Kentucky Derby after I finished working on the book, and we had a picture taken with him and me and the trophy he always felt he should have won. I kid him that he got more votes than the best damn football player ever to lace them up...Jim Brown. There has never been another year that produced a list of top 10 Heisman finishers like 1956:

1. Paul Hornung—(Notre Dame) College and Pro Football Halls of Fame
2. Johnny Majors—(Tennessee) College and Pro Football Halls of Fame
3. Tom McDonald—(Oklahoma) College and Pro Football Halls of Fame
4. Jim Parker—(Ohio State) College and Pro Football Halls of Fame
5. Jim Brown—(Syracuse) College and Pro Football Halls of Fame
6. Ron Kramer—(Michigan) College Football Hall of Fame
7. Jerry Tubbs—(Oklahoma) College Football Hall of Fame
8. Jon Arnett—(Southern Cal) College Football Hall of Fame
9. Len Dawson—(Purdue) College and Pro Football Halls of Fame
10. John Brodie—(Stanford) College Football Hall of Fame

As you can see, every player in the top 10 from the Heisman voting in 1956 is in the College Football Hall of Fame, and six are in the Pro Football Hall of Fame. After Jim Brown ended up fifth, my good friend Dick Schaap protested by never voting again.

Sports fans love to argue about who's the best: who's the best quarterback, linebacker, running back, and so on. Although there are objective measurements, it usually comes down to a subjective judgment, and here are my personal selections of the greatest players from my era.

First, let's look at the quarterbacks. From 1956 to 1960 I saw Norm Van Brocklin, one of the greatest arms ever. Then there was Y. A. Tittle, who threw 36 touchdown passes in 1963, which was a record, and of course the great Bobby Layne. Bobby may not have been the greatest on the field, but he spent more money partying than any other player

The 1956 Heisman Trophy race stands head and shoulders above any other year, before or since, with the great Jim Brown finishing a modest fifth. Photo courtesy of AP/Wide World Photos.

in history. One thing is for certain. If any other quarterback ever went with Bobby every day, they wouldn't have a chance. Layne would be the best. Bobby made me and Max McGee look like amateurs. He liked to drink...and drink, but he is still recognized as a College and Pro football Hall of Famer.

In the same era we had John Unitas and Bart Starr, Sonny Jurgensen and Fran Tarkenton. Most sportswriters at that time would have selected John Unitas as the best. We had some great games against the Colts, and Bart Starr's record in those years is unmatched. We were 9–1 in the playoffs with five championships, including the first two Super Bowls, and Bart Starr was the MVP of both. Bart's record is impeccable. Of course, I'm prejudiced, but I have to be loyal to the Packers, and Bart was our man.

In any discussion of quarterbacks, you can't leave out Otto Graham. He was fantastic for Paul Brown, who is hailed as one of the forces that led the NFL into the modern era, but I was never a big fan of Otto Graham as a player. I never got along with him after he coached us in the All-Star Game in Chicago in 1957. He had three quarterbacks for that game, John Brodie, Len Dawson, and myself. A week before the game on Saturday night, Jon Arnett and I went to the Chez Parez nightclub in Chicago with dates. We knew we were going to be late and miss the 11:00 PM curfew, but we felt safe because we ran into the head coach of the All-Star team that year, Curly Lambeau. Curly, who was escorting actress Jane Russell, saw us, came over, and said, "Don't say anything about seeing me, and I'll do the same."

This was nine days before the game, and somehow Otto Graham found out. Even though more than half the team missed curfew that night, the only two players he checked were Jim Brown and me. So you can have Otto Graham as far as I'm concerned, but as a player he was one of the great ones. Fortunately, he played before my time.

People can argue about who the best quarterback ever is, but in any such argument, the answer is not one of the guys already mentioned,

People can argue about the best quarterback of all time and never come to a definitive conclusion. But the most popular? Without question, it was Broadway Joe. Photo courtesy of AP/Wide World Photos.

and it's not Montana, or Favre, or Marino either. Joe Namath wins that one hands down. Broadway Joe predicted the win for his Jets in Super Bowl III when the Unitas-led Colts were 19-point favorites. I know the exact spread because I bet on the Colts. Namath's prediction was sensationalized by the press, which had nothing else much to write about in an otherwise boring run-up to the game. I have always felt this was the most important game in my lifetime. It saved the AFL, and Namath was named MVP.

For 13 years, I hosted my television show, *The Paul Hornung Sports Showcase*. Every week I had a special guest, ranging from people like Brett Favre and Bart Starr to Pete Rose and Oscar Robertson...the old and the new. Joe Namath was the most popular with the crowd. My wife, Angela, was very impressed with Joe because of the way he responded to the people. He talked with everyone, took pictures with everyone, and gave autographs to everyone. He was fantastic with the fans. At Canton, Ohio, when Joe is introduced, he always gets the biggest ovation and the loudest reception from the crowd, no matter who is being inducted.

I once offered Joe $500,000 to do a TV show in New York. I told him we would pattern it after my show, but his presence would make the difference. We were going to call it *Namath on Broadway* and would do the show from a very popular restaurant called Gallagher's on 52nd and Broadway. I planned a 13-week run and promised Joe by the end of two years we would split at least $2 million. I wanted to get behind the camera as a producer, and Joe liked the idea, but he was going through a divorce at the time and didn't want to spend that much time away from his young daughters.

The following players were standouts and Hall of Famers in my day in the NFL: Jim Brown, Cleveland Browns; Gale Sayers, Chicago Bears; Dick Butkus, Chicago Bears; Ray Nitschke, Green Bay Packers; Jim Parker, Baltimore Colts; Forrest Gregg, Green Bay Packers; Mike Ditka, Chicago Bears; Lenny Moore, Baltimore Colts; Jim Taylor, Green Bay Packers; Joe Schmidt, Detroit Lions; Bart Starr, Green Bay Packers; Alex Karras, Detroit Lions; John Unitas, Baltimore Colts; Doug Atkins, Chicago Bears; Sonny Jurgensen, Washington Redskins; Gino Marchetti, Baltimore Colts; Deacon Jones, Los Angeles Rams; Yale Lary, Detroit Lions; Chuck Bednarik, Philadelphia Eagles; Tommy McDonald, Philadelphia Eagles/Los Angeles Rams; Coach Vince Lombardi, Green Bay Packers; and Owner/Coach George Halas, Chicago Bears.

I think that the following men are the best of the best.

Jim Brown. Brown is the consensus choice for the best player in the history of the National Football League. But he will always remember Green Bay, because we handled him maybe better than anyone ever had in the three or four times we met. In the 1965 championship game, Nitschke and company held him to under 100 yards rushing, while I gained 107 yards and scored the winning touchdown as we won our third championship.

Dick Butkus. I used to kid Ray Nitschke that even though he was named best middle linebacker in the first 50 years of the NFL, he was only the second best to come out of Illinois! Both he and Butkus were from Illinois. Nitschke didn't like my kidding too much, and I thought he was going to kick my ass, but thank God he didn't.

Gale Sayers. He played only three and a half years on two good legs, and he was the most exciting runner I've ever seen. If he had been able to play 10 years in great shape with good knees, I firmly believe he would have been the best of all time. If you saw Sayers play when he was healthy, consider yourself lucky.

Vince Lombardi. I can't say much more than has already been said about the best coach in the history of the NFL. My teammates and I were so very lucky to have been in Green Bay during his time. He was simply the best.

George Halas. There was no finer competitor. Lombardi loved George Halas and respected his leadership in all the years he led the Chicago Bears. I always wanted to play in Chicago, but not after Vince arrived in Green Bay. I loved it when Halas cussed me out during a game. You knew you were special if he was hollering and cursing at you. I once told him I would rather play and beat the Bears than do anything else in life, and I know Vince Lombardi felt the same way.